"Heads up! That's Saedi Bocci's shout out to teens and their par[ents] screens and live. The simple and sensible strategies in *The Social* will help teens and parents do just that. Highly recommended."

> —**Michael A. Tompkins, PhD, ABPP**, codirector of the San Francisco Bay Area Center for Cognitive Therapy; assistant clinical professor at the University of California, Berkeley; and coauthor of *The Relaxation and Stress Reduction Workbook for Teens*

"This book is for typical teens (and adults) who frequently experience FOMO, stress, low self-esteem, and sadness when using social media. The book offers simple steps for choosing when and how to use social media. This book will support you in finding more happiness and freedom both online and IRL."

> —**Amy Saltzman, MD**, author of *A Still Quiet Place for Teens*

"A helpful and realistic resource for navigating an increasingly complicated world!"

> —**Christopher Willard**, author of *Growing Up Mindful*, and faculty member at Harvard Medical School

"Saedi Bocci provides a thoughtful, detailed, and considerate approach to a timely and challenging topic. She offers a rational and clinically informed approach to behavior change when coping with the 'downsides' of social media and its unintended, psychologically invasive consequences. The book provides an overview and detailed self-help manual for young readers (including parents) to learn about the problem, to examine their own behaviors with social media, and to gain a better understanding of how it can profoundly influence their lives. More generally, Saedi Bocci supplies a template for future research to evaluate the optimal means of addressing these expanding concerns about the adverse effects of social media upon younger—and probably also older—individuals."

> —**Scott M. Monroe,** William K. Warren Foundation professor in the department of psychology at the University of Notre Dame

"Teens need this book! *The Social Media Workbook for Teens* is an excellent resource that promotes mindful device use and social media participation. The book is user-friendly with deep, guiding questions for teens needing to balance their online presence with off-line recreational activities and face-to-face interactions. The book fills teens' toolboxes with tips, a process for creating action and backup plans, as well as the encouragement of self-care."

> —**Joanne Broder, PhD**, former president of the Society for Media Psychology and Technology, device management and intelligence; editor of *Psychology of Popular Media Culture*; and author of *Finish Your Dissertation, Don't Let it Finish You!*

the social media workbook for teens

---

skills to help you balance screen time, manage stress & take charge of your life

GOALI SAEDI BOCCI, PhD

Instant Help Books
An Imprint of New Harbinger Publications, Inc.

Publisher's Note

This publication is designed to provide accurate and authoritative information in regard to the subject matter covered. It is sold with the understanding that the publisher is not engaged in rendering psychological, financial, legal, or other professional services. If expert assistance or counseling is needed, the services of a competent professional should be sought.

In consideration of evolving American English usage standards, and reflecting a commitment to equity for all genders, "they/them" is used in this book to denote singular persons.

Trademarks owned by third parties are used in this book pursuant to the Fair Use Doctrine. No sponsorship or endorsement by, and no affiliation with, the trademark owner(s) are claimed or implied by the author or publisher.

Distributed in Canada by Raincoast Books

Cover design by Amy Shoup

Acquired by Wendy Millstine

Edited by Karen Shader

Library of Congress Cataloging-in-Publication Data on file

21   20   19

10   9   8   7   6   5   4   3   2   1   First Printing

To the teens and families who have opened up their lives and worlds to me, I am infinitely grateful. You are the reason this book even exists!

To my parents for encouraging me from my early years through my teens and well beyond to living out my dream of being a psychologist and writer.

To my husband, Bret, for always believing.

Contents

Section I: De-Friending Your Devices

Section II: Applicable Survival Skills

Section III: Going Tech-Free

When I was seventeen, which was eons ago, AOL had just gone mainstream. Every time I used my dial-up modem, a loud screeching sound would indicate its connection to the service. A lot has changed since 1996! Today, social media and smartphones provide us with instantaneous connection to our friends, news, and information on almost any topic—it's like carrying a set of encyclopedias and all your friends in your pocket to hang out with anytime you want. Having these services and the information they provide is amazing and astounding, but maintaining a healthy balance is imperative—and knowing that tipping point of when social media use becomes excessive or hits an unhealthy level is crucial.

It comes down to self-responsibility. As with any privilege (yes, that is right—a phone is a privilege, not a right), you have to consider its safety, overuse, and misuse. Consider the privilege of driving a car. You learn the rules of the road, get a driver's license, and use a car responsibly—otherwise there are serious consequences. Similarly, with social media and time spent on devices, there are many times when we can push the limits too far—this applies not only to teens, but to adults as well. That is right: this book can be used for both teens and adults. I know many parents and adult friends of mine who could greatly benefit from becoming aware of and intentional about their screen time, and from learning other healthy strategies that this book provides. I consider how using my own screen time sometimes cuts into my sleep and face-to-face time with people, pets, and nature. Yes, it's true. I am not perfect; no one is, and this book isn't prescribing any of us to be perfect with our devices. It is about being aware, responsible, and balanced with our use.

Dr. Goali Saedi Bocci provides clear steps for becoming aware of, managing, and supporting your social media use. Dr. Saedi Bocci provides readers with accessible and attainable steps to balance screen time, manage stress, and take charge of your life. She doesn't suggest not using your devices or to stop engaging in social media; rather, as with any other privilege, she suggests that you consider your responsibility for using it without excess. She challenges us to consider what we might be missing out on when we are constantly online.

There are three sections to this book. First, De-friending Your Devices is about learning to reduce possible dependency on devices. Second, *App*licable Survival Skills is focused on being empowered to move between the virtual and the real world with balance.

Third, Going Tech-Free involves learning about potential hobbies In Real Life (IRL), and using this newfound time to delve into self-growth and personal development.

What I love most about this book is the wealth of actionable activities. In this book, you will learn how to nourish your body; set healthy boundaries; engage in positive coping skills; reduce stress and anxiety; and increase self-compassion, mindfulness, and acceptance. And these are just a few of the things you will learn. There are a myriad of hands-on interventions from two researched and evidence-based programs: Cognitive Behavioral Therapy (CBT) and Mindfulness-Based Interventions (MBIs).

With a car, you don't need to know how to put an engine together or all the different interworkings of a chassis to drive it, but it sure is useful to know when your gas tank is getting low, or when you need to put air in your tires. It is important to be an educated user, not merely a passive observer and receiver of information. What is behind the screen? Regardless of which site you are on, it is being tracked by advertisers, potentially hundreds of them. These advertisers are gleaning your information behind the scenes. For example, on almost any web browser you can go to the developer mode and see which advertisers are acquiring information and resources about you—your demographics, interests, purchasing style, time on the site, location, and the like. This information is then sold to companies that use it to target you and others in your demographic. When you surf the web or post on social media, you don't see what is going on behind the scenes.

Here's another example: consider someone who signs up and gets on social media when they are thirteen years old and posts around ten times per day. By the time they are twenty, they will have made 25,550 posts in seven years. Behind the scenes, this information is taken and used to benefit big businesses. This isn't to say there aren't wonderful benefits to having the world at your fingertips. However, if you are only experiencing your life and world through a screen, you are missing out on living your life as it unfolds moment to moment. This is living life mindfully with intention and purpose. Living your life as if it really mattered. Don't have FOMO. Live IRL!

> —Gina M. Biegel, MA, LMFT, psychotherapist, researcher; author, and
> coauthor of several books including *Be Mindful and Stress Less*, *Mindfulness for Student Athletes*, and *The Stress Reduction Workbook for Teens*

to the parents and professionals reading this book

It seems impossible these days to go anywhere without seeing someone on their phone. Whether it's waiting in line to pick up a coffee order or sitting in an airport terminal, as humans we can't seem to overcome the urge to check. We check for text messages, alerts for likes on photos, and to see whether someone responded to our post. If we're not socially connecting with others, then we're checking the weather, searching the internet, online shopping, thumbing through our playlist, or doing any of the other millions of things our phones enable us to do.

Though one of the most brilliant inventions of our time, smartphones have also quickly become one of the most problematic tools for digital natives and the adults who care deeply about their well-being. The constant pinging of our devices has been shown scientifically to increase our anxiety. A direct source for connecting with friends and peers, social media has also made bullying, interpersonal aggression, and hostility more ubiquitous than ever. We can send messages that instantaneously delete themselves, erasing any proof of the harm that others may have done to us or that we have inflicted upon others.

Social media has also allowed us to have public and private selves that we may selectively share with friends and family. We can have secondary Instagram accounts where we play with the prospect of another identity entirely. At an age when teens are finding themselves, the idea of a fake profile may be thrilling, as is the ability to connect with new strangers across the globe. However, virtual connections can quickly escalate and become problematic, and teens may not know how to handle uncomfortable situations or whom to reach out to for help. Stressors can abound.

Finally, for teens struggling with any host of emotional or physical concerns, social media can further aggravate difficulties. Teens with depression or anxiety may be bombarded by a barrage of images that exacerbate their concerns. Teens who have struggled with self-injurious behaviors may follow self-harm profiles that further trigger them each time they log on to their social media. As teens can be highly empathic toward friends with similar concerns, they may find themselves staying up all night trying to console friends through text. They may succeed in comforting a hurting friend only to plunge deeper into depression or anxiety themselves.

According to research conducted in 2018 by the Pew Research Center, 45 percent of teens are online "almost constantly," and this is facilitated through the widespread availability of smartphones; 91 percent of teens go online from a mobile device at least occasionally. As such, the aims of this workbook are threefold. Given that phones are the primary devices upon which social media is accessed, the first goal is to reduce both screen time on the phone and social media usage at large. Although a number of skills are introduced to facilitate reduced dependency on devices, the second goal is to empower teens to move out of the virtual world into the real world. Although much happens virtually in the teen world, being glued to a phone can lead them to miss some incredible opportunities. Teens may miss out on amazing trips and excursions or simply heart-to-heart conversations with friends in person. Furthermore, the teenage years are some of the foundational times for trying new hobbies, sports, art, music, and social initiatives. Therefore the third goal of this book is to empower teens to develop new hobbies, be more physically active, and delve into self-growth and personal development. Tools for managing anxiety and coping skills are also provided to help teens embark upon this new terrain confidently and with excitement.

In the pages that follow, I encourage teens and those guiding them through this workbook—whether parents, educators, or therapists—to embrace a curiosity about what life holds when we lift our eyes up from our screens.

to the teens reading this book

Chances are that in this very moment your phone is within five feet of you, if not much closer. In fact, this rings true for most of us. Let's face it—our phones are our lifelines. They allow us to call our parents to pick us up from school when we're not feeling well, and they are the way we connect with all our friends. A life without phones can seem unimaginable. And I would have to agree with you on that. After all, how else would we wake up on time, snap photos instantaneously, and share how we are feeling with our friends? But in working with a lot of teens, I have learned this: even though teens love keeping in touch with friends through text messages and social media, they also absorb a lot of stress, angst, and drama from their friends this way.

Many times, communicating with friends through social media or text messages can be positive. Friends might compliment a photo you posted or send you an uplifting message when you are having a rough day. However, the social landscape can shift quickly. Someone who might have been a friend one day is now posting mean things about you or others. Possibly worse yet, people you've never even met can cyberbully you, and life just gets a whole lot more complicated than it needs to be. On top of the regular stress of trying to keep up with school, sports, and other activities, social stressors only make things worse. Challenges with friends can make you feel alone, isolated, or frustrated. Phones and computers can make this worse as disagreements can escalate far more quickly through messages and posts than they would otherwise. You might pick up your phone to see dozens of messages in the time it took you to walk to the refrigerator to get a snack.

The good news is that it doesn't have to be this way. Perhaps this book was given to you by a parent, teacher, or therapist. Maybe they have expressed worries about how much time you spend on your phone or other devices. Or they notice you being more agitated or stressed after spending time checking your social media. Either way, this book is intended to help you learn to manage such stressors and take a step back from all the time spent being digitally connected. When teens take a break from their devices, they find not only that life still moves on but also that they have more perspective and less anxiety. They are able to focus better in school and truly take in positive experiences such as family vacations and celebrations. They also see that much of the drama they have been worrying about resolves itself and only serves to bring about negative energy.

Believe it or not, many of the teens I've worked with have secretly shared that sometimes when their parents have forced them to put down their devices or taken them away, it's been a relief. But it shouldn't have to come down to this either. Ideally, you can learn to manage these things on your own. After all, that's part of becoming an adult!

In this workbook, you will be introduced to a number of activities aimed at helping you decrease your stress and scale back your usage of phones and other devices. Through enlisting the support of family (Activity 7) and friends (Activity 8), you will learn to set boundaries (Activity 9) and learn to identify stressful thoughts and combat them (Activities 11 and 12). Learning to take care of yourself through getting good sleep (Activity 17) and exercise (Activity 19) will be encouraged, because these are the building blocks of wellness. You will learn to practice self-care (Activity 21) and nourish your soul (Activity 23) while experimenting with going tech-free for a weekend (Activity 27). You might be surprised to find how much sweeter life becomes when you don't have the chronic stress of attending to your virtual life and start living your real one.

Section I

De-Friending Your Devices

1 do I really have a problem with social media?

for you to know

Many of us struggle with setting limits on any problematic behavior. Though we can sometimes be quick to label things an "addiction" or "obsession," this labeling doesn't mean it's true in the clinical sense. However, problematic behaviors don't have to reach a diagnosable level to be serious.

Given how common it is these days to see everyone on their devices, online and connecting with friends, it may not seem that your behaviors are problematic in any way. After all, isn't that what the teenage years are all about? Perhaps your friends' parents have given them a hard time about their social media use or maybe they are really relaxed about it. Either way, you might not be certain whether you even have a problem with social media.

directions

Take the self-assessment quiz on the next page to learn more about your relationship with social media usage. Be as open and honest as you can about your responses. Many times we will change our responses because we want to see things as we'd like them to be rather than as they really are. Try not to overthink the options, and simply go with what feels right.

When you've finished, go over your answers and score your self-assessment. Give yourself 1 for each time you marked "very rarely," 2 for every response of "rarely," 3 for each time you said "sometimes," 4 for "often," and 5 for "very often." Add up your points. If you scored somewhere between 24 and 30, you may have a more serious issue with social media than you initially realized.

You spend a lot of time thinking about social media or planning how to use it.

☐ Very rarely   ☐ Rarely   ☐ Sometimes   ☐ Often   ☐ Very often

Score: _____

You feel an urge to use social media more and more.

☐ Very rarely   ☐ Rarely   ☐ Sometimes   ☐ Often   ☐ Very often

Score: _____

You use social media in order to forget about personal problems.

☐ Very rarely   ☐ Rarely   ☐ Sometimes   ☐ Often   ☐ Very often

Score: _____

You have tried to cut down on the use of social media without success.

☐ Very rarely   ☐ Rarely   ☐ Sometimes   ☐ Often   ☐ Very often

Score: _____

You become restless or troubled if you are prohibited from using social media.

☐ Very rarely   ☐ Rarely   ☐ Sometimes   ☐ Often   ☐ Very often

Score: _____

You use social media so much that it has had a negative impact on your job or studies.

☐ Very rarely   ☐ Rarely   ☐ Sometimes   ☐ Often   ☐ Very often

Score: _____

Total score: _____

more to do...

After completing your self-assessment, consider sharing this exercise with two or three trusted friends and have them take the quiz as well. Then, consider having a conversation about your social media usage as a group. Use this experience as an opportunity to discuss the following questions and record your responses below.

What were your overall impressions of your total score? Were you surprised to find you scored higher or lower than you may have initially guessed?

_____

_____

_____

_____

Did any of the questions stand out to you? Why?

_____

_____

_____

_____

Discuss how reliance on social media or technology may be a problem within your friend group.

_____

_____

_____

_____

How can you help support one another to have a healthier relationship with your devices?

_____

_____

_____

_____

_____

_____

2 living in the present or on your feed?

for you to know

Like most habits, the problematic ones are often those that we notice the least. Perhaps there is a family member or friend who habitually engages in some form of harmful behavior without realizing it. Or maybe they are aware but are struggling to make changes or find help. The first step can often involve loved ones providing their observations and positive support.

"You're always on your phone!"

"Will you put that thing down for a minute!"

"You're addicted to your phone."

Perhaps these are common refrains you have heard from parents, extended family, teachers, or even friends. But when you look around, these concerns may seem exaggerated. Your friend Josh sleeps with his phone under his pillow. Sara showers with her phone nearby in the bathroom. From your perspective, it might seem that they are the ones with concerning behaviors, not you. It can be challenging to understand the concerns of friends and family because you are aware that it could be much worse. You might also think that others don't understand the urgency of replying to friends or how you will be left out of the loop by not communicating through your devices.

Think about a time when you had some type of concerning behavior that you were oblivious to. Maybe you were mindlessly picking at your hair or skin or grinding your teeth in your sleep. It's possible you were anxious and not even aware of what was going on. It wasn't until a friend pointed out blood on your face or a parent mentioned your teeth grinding that you realized there was something to be concerned about. Many times these second-nature habits can fly under our radar and we don't even question them. We don't realize we are engaging in a problematic behavior until someone tells us about it. That's where it can be helpful to get the perspective of trusted friends and adults. They can help us gain insight into concerning behaviors and areas for improvement.

directions

Find three people you trust (including at least one adult) and ask if you might be able to interview them about your device-related behaviors. Ask them to be honest, and have an open mind about their responses.

Interviewee #1:

Name: _____   Relationship to you: _____

How would you describe my relationship with my phone? With social media?

_____

_____

What (if any) behaviors regarding my usage are concerning?

_____

_____

_____

What percentage of the time would you say you observe me on my phone, other electronic device, or social media?

_____

Do I often seem distracted or like I am not really present with others?

_____

_____

Is my screen time problematic? _____

_____

Interviewee #2:

Name: _____   Relationship to you: _____

How would you describe my relationship with my phone? With social media?

_____

_____

What (if any) behaviors regarding my usage are concerning?

_____

_____

_____

What percentage of the time would you say you observe me on my phone, other electronic device, or social media?

_____

Do I often seem distracted or like I am not really present with others?

_____

_____

Is my screen time problematic? _____

_____

Interviewee #3:

Name: _____   Relationship to you: _____

How would you describe my relationship with my phone? With social media?

_____

_____

What (if any) behaviors regarding my usage are concerning?

_____

_____

_____

What percentage of the time would you say you observe me on my phone, other electronic device, or social media?

_____

Do I often seem distracted or like I am not really present with others?

_____

_____

Is my screen time problematic? _____

_____

more to do...

After you complete the interviews, take some time to reflect upon the answers these people provided.

Share which answers from the interviews surprised you the most.

_____

_____

_____

_____

Was there any feedback you particularly agreed or disagreed with? What makes you agree or disagree with this particular feedback?

_____

_____

_____

What do you think is a small way you can start making a change to be more present to those around you (for example, not having your phone at the dinner table, putting your devices away during family movie time)? If you have more than one idea, list them all here:

_____

_____

_____

_____

social media culprits 3

for you to know

Seventy-one percent of teens report using more than one type of social media platform. Examining the types of media that take up the most amount of your time can be a great first step in determining what changes to make.

When we talk about social media, we are immediately aware of what a wide array of apps, platforms, and mediums we are talking about. For each teen, their relationship with social media is different. Maybe they focus all their time on one platform, such as Facebook, or divide their attention between three different apps. Or they use one app, such as Instagram, with multiple profiles. To help you and those supporting you with modifying your social media usage, it can be useful to sit down and look at what the biggest culprits are.

directions

Below are some of the most commonly used social media apps. Check off any you use, and put an X by those you use daily or predominantly. Use the blank line to add any others:

____ Instagram	____ Snapchat	____ Twitter	____ Tumblr
____ Facebook	____ WhatsApp	____ Pinterest	____ Musical.ly
____ LinkedIn	____ YouTube	____ My Fitness Pal	

Other: _____

Do you have multiple profiles on any of these sites? If so, which platforms and how many profiles?

_____

_____

_____

As you look at all these forms of social media, are there ones that have lost some interest for you or that you rarely use? Would you consider deleting the app altogether or removing your account?

_____

_____

_____

12

more to do...

Many teens use app trackers to log time spent online and discover how much any one app is used. Apps such as Moment or built-in features like Screen Time can tell you how much time you spend on your phone and even help you start to limit your time on your device. You can preset a designated amount of time so that once you reach a certain limit, you are no longer able to access your apps. Consider downloading such an app and gathering data on your usage over the next week. Record your findings here:

_____

_____

_____

_____

_____

_____

4   daily tracking log

for you to know

It can be easy to lose track of time, especially with the busy lives teens lead. Between homework and sports and trying to find time for friends and family, you may feel like you are always behind. Although you may have a general sense of where your time goes, tracking it can be particularly illuminating to help you see where your time sinks are.

Most teens are already familiar with the concept of a daily planner or agenda. Sometimes they use one to write down assignments, and other times they just track appointments and commitments. While some prefer to structure such planners on a daily basis, others find an hour-by-hour analysis to be most helpful so they don't get off track. In this activity, you'll use an hourly tracking method to help you see where your time goes on a daily basis, with an emphasis on also examining how much time is spent on the computer, phone, or other device. Mood tracking is particularly common in many types of therapy and can help you see how your mood may fluctuate on a daily or weekly basis. Using this framework, you will track both your daily activities and your mood to see whether a pattern arises.

Perhaps some of your friends have already started tracking their time in a similar way. Maybe your friend Gracie relies on an hourly agenda to get her from volleyball practice to piano to after-school tutoring. Without a way to track her obligations, she would run the risk of mixing up appointments and not getting to places promptly. She might even limit her time on Facebook or other social media by having a timer that keeps her from browsing for too long. On the other hand, you might have friends like Taylor, who doesn't use any type of planner. These friends often hand in assignments late, are confused about where they need to be, and are overall frazzled and stressed. They may lament always losing track of time and never getting anything done.

Making a schedule and seeing where our time goes can be highly informative and save us precious hours. For example, if you start realizing that every night you lose two to three hours on your phone, you might be able to allocate that time to painting that canvas you've been meaning to complete.

directions

Use the chart on the next page (or download a copy at http://www.newharbinger .com/41900) to track your daily activities starting from the morning all the way until you go to bed at night. Although most of your school week will involve sitting in class, be sure to also track the time between classes, when you're talking to friends or using your phone or other screens. Many schools require computers for certain classes; include required use in your tracking so you get an overall total of how much time a day is spent looking at a screen. Include any time watching television shows after school on any sort of device as well. At the end of each day, rate your overall mood on a scale from 1 (terrible) to 10 (excellent).

	Mon	Tues	Wed	Thurs	Fri	Sat	Sun
6:00 a.m.							
7:00 a.m.							
8:00 a.m.							
9:00 a.m.							
10:00 a.m.							
11:00 a.m.							
Noon							
1:00 p.m.							
2:00 p.m.							
3:00 p.m.							
4:00 p.m.							
5:00 p.m.							
6:00 p.m.							
7:00 p.m.							
8:00 p.m.							
9:00 p.m.							
10:00 p.m.							
11:00 p.m.							
Midnight							
Total hours on screen							
Mood rating (1 = terrible; 10 = excellent)							

more to do...

Spend some time reflecting on your findings from your week of tracking your activities and mood.

What stood out to you the most about your overall experience of this tracking?

_____

_____

_____

_____

What were your best days? Why?

_____

_____

_____

What were your worst days? What do you think contributed to this?

_____

_____

_____

What behaviors do you think you could change to improve your overall mood and day?

_____

_____

_____

5 stages of change

Making any type of change can feel scary and disorienting. Although we may sometimes have an idea of what we'd like to change, sometimes we don't even know where to begin. In 1992, clinical psychologists James Prochaska and Carlo DiClemente developed a useful framework to help you understand the stages of making change. Their "stages of change" model explains the different steps involved in making a lasting change. These include *precontemplation*, *contemplation*, *preparation*, *action*, and *maintenance*.

In the *precontemplation* stage, it is common for individuals to be completely unaware that there is any sort of problematic behavior. An example is teens who may text and drive. They might not see texting and driving as problematic at all, so they don't even realize they need to change their behavior.

In the *contemplation* stage, individuals know they have some sort of problem and start thinking about whether they want to make a change. For example, let's say the teen driver who is texting and driving nearly rear-ends a car while texting. It scares them, and they start considering that maybe they shouldn't be texting and driving.

The *preparation* stage involves gathering resources and tools and setting a date for a behavior change. Perhaps the teen puts their phone on airplane mode and picks a day to enact this change. They might tell their parents they will text when they arrive at their destination, or think of places they can pull over on their route if they must text someone back. Preparation is an important step in the process, as it sets the stage for success.

During the *action* stage, the desired behavior change is finally enacted. The teen puts their phone on do not disturb mode, out of sight, and lets everyone know they will not be available when behind the wheel. The behaviors are finally in full swing!

Maintenance involves continually reinforcing or acting to keep up the behavior. We have all started new goals only to drop them a week later. In maintenance, we may introduce periodic rewards to sustain the behavior. For example, the teen driver might buy a new phone case or purchase music as a reward for not texting and driving. The maintenance stage can be quite dynamic and customized to fit the individual's goals and unique circumstances.

directions

Think about a behavior you might want to change. It can relate to your social media or screen usage, or even involve general health goals. Write down your goal—the behavior you'd like to change—here:

_____

_____

_____

_____

Using the flow chart below, check where you are in the stages of change model and fill in what the next steps might look like. Chances are that if you have stated a goal, you have already moved past the *precontemplation* stage, so congratulations on that! You don't have to worry about springing into action; just brainstorming what the next stages might look like can help move you in that direction.

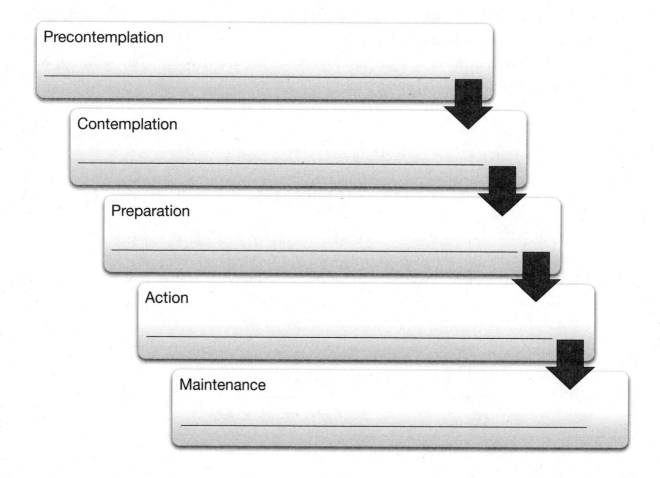

Precontemplation

_____

Contemplation

_____

Preparation

_____

Action

_____

Maintenance

_____

more to do...

Using the goal you wrote down, think about what the next stage looks like for you. Perhaps you were in the contemplation stage, considering deleting some social media apps or starting an exercise regimen. Below, list three steps you can take in the coming week that might move you toward the next corresponding stage (in the examples stated here, it would be preparation).

_____

_____

_____

Now, see if you can implement these steps. After a week or so, consider if you might be ready to move on to the next stage, and return to this page in your workbook. If you feel ready, list the next stage here: _____. Then, list three more steps that might move you to the next stage and see if you can implement those steps as well:

_____

_____

_____

6 goal setting for change

for you to know

Setting goals can be challenging for the most determined of teens. Many teens quickly find that meeting their goals can be harder than they anticipate, whether they're New Year's resolutions, summer goals to read more books, or plans to start on homework earlier. However, it turns out that not all goals are created equally.

Think about the last time you set an intention for change and succeeded. Now think about all those times you fell short of your goal. What was different about each scenario? Perhaps you were more naturally motivated toward one goal or set up smaller steps to accomplish it. Many times, if we have a goal that is too general or open-ended, we may get overwhelmed and lose our drive altogether. If our goal is too narrowly defined or too simple, we may not grow or be challenged as much as we'd like to be.

A commonly used framework for setting up goals is called SMART goals, which stands for *specific, measurable, attainable, realistic,* and *time-bound*. Because many of us have a tendency to set goals that are too broadly defined, we often may not know how to begin working toward them. The SMART framework helps protect against this by encouraging us to get the maximum amount of clarity and definition possible when setting goals. On the next page is an example of a typical goal a teen might set versus a SMART goal.

Typical Goal: To get in shape

SMART Goal:

    Specific: I will begin getting in shape through training for a 5K.

    Measurable: I will run three times a week for thirty minutes.

    Attainable: I am currently in good enough shape to start with a slow jog and then advance to running more quickly. There are also many 5K runs in the area where I live.

    Realistic: I will compete in a 5K after six months of regular jogging. Competing in a full marathon may not be as realistic at this point.

    Time-bound: I plan to reach my goal of getting in shape and running a 5K by training three times a week for thirty minutes at a time over a span of six months.

Although it takes more work to produce a SMART goal, making the effort to become more concrete about your intentions significantly increases your chances for success. You also are more aware of potential pitfalls to watch out for.

directions

Take some time to think about what your goals may be with respect to changing your social media and screen-related behaviors. Perhaps you tried in the past with more general goals such as "I'll use my phone less," or "I'll turn off my phone during dinner," but did not find this very effective. Whether your goals involve computer usage, gaming, or reducing texting and driving, it's important to set some concrete goals for yourself. As you work your way through this book, you can then refer back to these goals.

Use the space that follows to complete two goals you'd like to work on. One might be related to your device usage and the other might include personal goals (for example, eating healthier, sleeping more) to help support your overall well-being.

SMART Goal #1: _____

    Specific: _____

    Measurable: _____

    Attainable: _____

    Realistic: _____

    Time-bound: _____

SMART Goal #2: _____

    Specific: _____

    Measurable: _____

    Attainable: _____

    Realistic: _____

    Time-bound: _____

more to do...

Now that you have set your two goals, pick one and put it into action! On your paper calendar or school planner, circle the date the desired behavior is supposed to occur by. Then, work backward and start implementing your goal one step at a time.

As an added motivator, you might announce this goal publicly. Although for many teens announcements naturally happen on social media, consider another way of making your declaration, such as writing it out on a page and posting it on the fridge or your bedroom door. Write this plan here:

_____

_____

_____

_____

To further help motivate yourself to stick to your new goal, you might choose to use what behavioral psychologists refer to as *positive reinforcement* (for example, eating a delicious slice of cake or watching that movie you've been wanting to see). Naturally, the best motivation comes from a feeling of accomplishment from within, but a little treat every now and again never hurt either! Below, list three positive reinforcements that might help you adhere to the goals you listed:

_____

_____

_____

7 creating family change

Many teens think that the very goals their parents are imposing on them are ones the parents themselves can benefit from working on. Maybe a parent keeps nagging you to put away your phone, even as they are on their device, reading a newspaper or book. It can be tough to see family members all highly connected to their screens while expecting you to make a change. It is for this reason that many therapists recommend creating a family culture of change.

If a family member is trying to lose weight, all members might have to suffer with newer healthy fare for dinner. Cookies might be hard to come by, and frustrations and resistance may arise. The same idea will likely apply to going on a device "diet" of sorts. Family members may not see any reason for changing their behaviors or may assume they have no problem with technology—or they might be so excited to see you spending less time on your devices that they gladly give up their own. Whatever the dynamic might be in your family, keep an open mind and remain optimistic!

directions

It might feel a bit unnerving at first to approach family members about giving up their devices and helping you in detaching from yours. After all, once you go public, going back becomes a lot harder. Taking some time to come up with a coherent agenda can help you feel confident about making your announcement and hopes for family change. To help you get started, fill out the chart below; you can also download a copy at http://www.newharbinger.com/41900.

You may only be able to fill out the first half, but it can get you ready for having a meeting where together you can brainstorm, create goals, and determine appropriate rewards.

Family Meeting Agenda

Date of meeting: _____ Time: _____

Location: _____

Introduction: _____
(Write down what you would say the goal of the meeting is—for example, discussing family tech troubles.)

(5–10 minutes)

Objective #1: _____
(Here you can fill out what your goal is for seeing family change—for example, a concrete change you'd like to see, such as no phones after 5:00 p.m.)

(5–10 minutes)

Objective #2: _____
(List the changes you are willing and planning to make related to device usage.)

(5–10 minutes)

Objective #3 (optional): _____

(List any additional changes in yourself and/or family members that could be positive and healthy.)

(10–15 minutes)

Open forum: _____

_____

(This forum is an opportunity for family members to weigh in, discuss, and express objections, concerns, or support and excitement. You can record their input here if you'd like.)

(5–10 minutes)

Brainstorm: _____

_____

(List ideas that come up regarding changes to make and how to make them.)

(10–15 minutes)

Resulting SMART Goals:

SMART Goal #1:

Specific: _____

Measurable: _____

Attainable: _____

Realistic: _____

Time-bound: _____

SMART Goal #2:

Specific: _____

Measurable: _____

Attainable: _____

Realistic: _____

Time-bound: _____
(5–10 minutes)

Reward for achieving goal(s): _____
(Come up with a list of possible family rewards such as pizza night or a camping trip.)

Adjourn meeting!

more to do...

Now that you have the agenda, you can put it into action! Approach your parents and ask if you might be able to call a family meeting, perhaps around the dinner table or maybe on a Friday evening when everyone is relaxing together. If you'd like to tell them ahead of time that it is about your technology-related goals, that works too. You might even get them to agree to having some fun snacks or ice cream to make it more light-hearted. You might choose to print out agendas for everyone or have a large poster board for writing your brainstorm list together. You can get as elaborate as you'd like.

Once you have held the meeting and come up with your goals, consider using the family technology tracker below to help keep you all accountable; you can also download a copy at http://www.newharbinger.com/41900. Write down the device-related goal. Specify whether it relates to a particular family member, you exclusively, or all of you by placing an X in the corresponding box. If it relates only to a single person, include that person's name. Then, for each day, rate on a scale of 1 to 10 how well each member did at attaining the goal (for example, if the goal was to use the phone for no more than an hour each day, maybe your little brother did well roughly 70 percent of the time; the rating would be 7). Ideally, you'll start using this tracker the day after your family meeting.

Goal:_____

Day	Individual family member	Yourself	Entire family
Sunday			
Monday			
Tuesday			
Wednesday			
Thursday			
Friday			
Saturday			

tapping your tech-free tribe   8

for you to know

Social support can be one of the most effective ways of making any type of change, as well as shielding us from the stressors of everyday life. Learning to enlist a strong circle of friends in enacting change can be very powerful. Having friends who are like-minded can be particularly helpful to us in not feeling alone in our struggles.

Like most teens, you probably find yourself hanging out with your friends while you are all typing away at your devices. Maybe you are sharing videos or pictures, or talking about what another friend just posted on social media. Whatever the activity may be, your phones are a major component of your active social life. As such, it might seem difficult to be the only one without a phone in hand. You might feel awkward or left out. However, there is a good chance your friends are also struggling with setting boundaries with their device usage. Even if they do not think they have a problem, good friends will support you in setting healthy goals for yourself. Although it may feel uncomfortable or scary to approach the idea of going off your phone for a while, communication is the first step in conveying your needs to your friends.

In therapy, we often talk about the idea of role-playing when we are trying to practice making changes that involve other people. For example, we might role-play a difficult conversation with a parent by practicing on our therapist first. Or maybe a friend helps you role-play asking someone you like to a school dance. While initially we may feel silly in such an exercise, it is one of the best ways of getting into the mind-set of having a real conversation involving difficult topics. Once we immerse ourselves in the exercise, we might realize that we are beating around the bush when we introduce the topic, or that we giggle uncomfortably. Practicing what we'll say is one of the best ways of becoming a more effective speaker.

directions

Below are several scripts for potential role-plays that involve expressing your intention to change your device-related behaviors. Because you will be eventually telling your friends about these changes, consider practicing in front of adults or individuals you feel safe with. You might even practice your speech in front of your dog! Fill in what you might say in each of these scenarios, and consider choosing someone to help you role-play to further elaborate or act out the scenario. That way, you can be prepared to answer any follow-up questions you get.

It is passing time between classes, and you want to begin a conversation regarding changing or reducing your phone usage. What might you say?

_____

_____

_____

You are on the school bus. Your friend is on their phone gaming, and you want to discuss reducing your gaming time. What might you say?

_____

_____

_____

At a slumber party, everyone is on their phone and you want to shift the conversation to something more serious. What might you say?

_____

_____

_____

more to do...

After spending some time going over various scenarios, taking the next step and actually having these conversations can be a powerful way to communicate your intention and decrease your anxiety.

Use the space that follows to list the close friends you need to have these conversations with. Next to each person's name, write down the scenario: when or where you can have this conversation. After you have the conversation, write down how it turned out. An example is provided to get you started.

Name: Juan

Scenario: On bus ride to football game

How it turned out: We were talking about the upcoming game while checking stats of our favorite sports teams on our phones. I casually brought up how I'm going to start following my favorite teams through magazines and newspapers instead of social media. Juan was surprised, but supportive overall.

Name: _____

Scenario: _____

How it turned out: _____

_____

_____

_____

Name: _____

Scenario: _____

How it turned out: _____

_____

_____

_____

Name: _____

Scenario: _____

How it turned out: _____

_____

_____

_____

Then, pick a day and share your plan to alter your device-related behaviors. After you have completed this activity, write down a summary of your friends' reactions:

_____

_____

_____

_____

_____

How do you feel now that you have shared your intentions with your friends? Do you feel more supported? Might this help decrease your anxiety about the need to always be connected to your phone or other device?

_____

_____

_____

_____

_____

_____

9 setting boundaries to save your sanity

for you to know

Setting healthy boundaries is key to the emotional well-being of any individual. Teens are often asked to give as much of their energy as they can in school, sports, and extracurricular activities, as well as at home. Learning to say no can be difficult, and in many instances those who do may be penalized. Practicing when to say no to additional pressures and how to care for oneself are important components of setting boundaries.

Think back to the last time you helped a friend in need. For many teens, this is a daily occurrence that happens over social media. They counsel friends who are struggling with peers or parents, or in school. In fact, many teens admit that they are the "therapist" in their friend group and that everyone comes to them for help. Even though helping friends through good listening and distractions is a wonderful skill, teens can also quickly get in over their heads. The same teens who admit to being the therapist to their friends also report becoming overwhelmed at times; when everyone reaches out to them for help, they do not know whom they can reach out to when in need.

Setting healthy boundaries involves learning when to lend an ear to a friend's woes and when to step back and let trusted adults and counselors intervene. Due to the nature of social media, it is often other teens who first learn that a friend is in emotional pain. Their natural response is to jump in and help. However, teens are not trained therapists and can quickly take on too much. Learning to listen and make an appropriate referral to a trusted adult is an important part of setting healthy boundaries.

directions

The list below provides some key elements of setting healthy boundaries with friends. Put a check next to the ones you already do and an X next to the ones you may need to work on incorporating.

_____ I tell my friends I am available to them when they are in need, but I understand this does not mean twenty-four-hour availability.

_____ I turn my phone and devices off at night and do not respond to "urgent" messages that may come in past my bedtime. If friends make a habit of doing this, I address this with them and kindly ask that they reach out to others or confide in an adult.

_____ I make a point of speaking up when I am feeling overwhelmed and do not take on the problems of others as my own.

_____ I know how to practice self-care and take care of myself when others are leaning on me for support.

_____ I am comfortable turning to trusted adults when helping friends takes a toll on me.

_____ I am able to turn off social media and other devices in the evening and make room for "me time" to recharge and reset.

_____ I feel comfortable talking to my parents when I feel overburdened with responsibilities.

more to do...

Reflect on your past challenges with setting boundaries with friends.

What did you find to be most difficult?

_____

_____

_____

_____

How might you work on enforcing firmer boundaries in the future?

_____

_____

_____

What might you say to friends to explain your need for firmer boundaries?

_____

_____

_____

How do you think that setting healthy boundaries can help your overall mental health?

_____

_____

_____

for you to know

Creating a list of pros and cons is a common approach for determining whether to pursue certain courses of action. Using such a list can help you recognize any uncertainties or fears you may have about making changes. It can also help clarify areas of uncertainty when you are forced to decide whether a factor has more positives or negatives.

Whether it's deciding to try out for varsity volleyball or what college to apply to, the idea of a pros and cons list may have been something you have already heard about. Although some people make the process more complicated by assigning numbers or weight to certain factors on the list, merely going through the process of creating one can be very helpful for anyone trying to make a big decision.

directions

Below is a sample list to help you brainstorm pros and cons. Use the blank spaces to add your own ideas.

Goal: Decreasing my social media usage

Pros	Cons
I won't be tempted to stay up late on my phone as much and might get better sleep as a result.	I won't be as up-to-date on everything going on with friends.
I won't get as stressed out keeping up with feeds on all my social media.	

Now create a pros and cons list based on the goals you set for yourself in Activity 6. You can download additional charts at http://www.newharbinger.com/41900.

Goal: _____

Pros	Cons

more to do...

Once they go through the process of writing down the pros and cons of adopting a new behavior, many teens find that the more pros there are, the easier it is to enact positive change. To continue reinforcing your new goal, consider the following visual representation. Find two mason jars (or cups, coffee cans, or other small containers); label one pros and the other cons. Collect a bunch of ice-pop sticks or even just slips of paper. As you begin implementing your goal and find new reasons to keep up the goal, write down these new reasons and put them in the pros jar. On tough days, you might write down a con and put it in the cons jar. Keep up with this exercise for a full month, and observe what happens. You may find one jar significantly fuller than the other! You can try this with additional goals you've set for yourself.

Section II

*App*licable Survival Skills

11 social media stress management

for you to know

While we learn many important skills for academic and career success, we are rarely taught the importance of stress management. Too often we are given unhelpful advice such as "just relax," without really being taught to battle our anxious thoughts in a concrete way. Learning to identify and analyze our thought distortions can be a powerfully helpful tool for managing our anxiety.

We have thousands of thoughts each day, and more often than not they can take on a negative tone. When we are running around busy with activities all day long or trying to meet the expectations of ourselves or others, our anxieties may flare. Many who have never experienced any anxiety are surprised by their body's strong reactions. Some experience panic attacks, racing heart, sweating, or racing thoughts. Others have simply accepted anxiety as a part of daily life and don't experience such reactions.

Because the world of social media is full of anxiety-provoking scenarios, learning to analyze our thoughts and see where they are traps for negative thinking can be a highly useful activity for any teen experiencing anxiety. Some of the most common thought distortions include the following:

black-and-white thinking
(also called all-or-nothing thinking)

This distortion means you don't see the shades of gray or alternative possibilities in a stressful circumstance.

Distortion: Your best friend doesn't respond to your text as quickly as usual, and you assume they no longer want to be your friend.

Reality: It's possible they ran out of battery on their phone and forgot their charger at home.

catastrophizing

This distortion involves looking only at the worst-case scenario.

Distortion: A friend posts an embarrassing photo or video of you, and you assume your reputation will be tainted forever.

Reality: It is human nature that over time people will forget about this post and move on to something new.

fortune telling (mind reading or predicting the future)

Distortion: Your girlfriend responded to your last message with one emoji when she is typically more expressive. You assume she has lost interest in you and is messaging other guys (mind reading). Your mind starts visualizing scenarios in which she is now breaking up with you (predicting the future).

Reality: You have no evidence for any of these conclusions. Rather, such distortions often mean your mind is filling in the blanks of a scenario in a negative way.

directions

Think about the last time a stressful scenario occurred on social media.

Describe the scenario here:

_____

_____

_____

_____

Now, see if you can identify whether any of the thought distortions you just read about applied to the situation. Is there a way that black-and-white thinking could have contributed to the experience?

_____

_____

How might catastrophizing have impacted the interaction?

_____

_____

Describe any way you might see fortune telling playing a role in this scenario:

_____

_____

more to do...

Over the next week, using the framework you just learned, see if you can start catching yourself when you think in these distortions. It can involve anxiety related to social media, or any other domain of your life causing distress. Perhaps you get anxious about a school test, or a public speech you must give. Learning to first identify the thought distortion and then turning it around to see reality can be incredibly powerful. Below is space for recording two stressful scenarios during the week.

Scenario: _____

    Distortion(s): _____

    Reality: _____

Scenario: _____

    Distortion(s): _____

    Reality: _____

In the next activity, you will learn more about additional thought distortions to build up your toolkit of social media stress-management skills.

12 dealing with device distress

for you to know

Managing our multiple devices is a stressor for most teens and adults. Parents may require that we be accessible by phone in case of emergencies, while schools may require computers and apps for completing homework in a timely manner. It can be challenging to learn how to limit our devices and the distress they can cause when they are such an integral part of life, but you can learn strategies to help you manage the burden better.

In the previous activity, you were introduced to the concept of thought distortions and how they may lead to much unnecessary anxiety in our lives. Although it is almost second nature to jump to these thinking traps, learning to become the master of our own minds can help us deal with our distress in a more effective way.

A few more of the most common types of thought distortions are listed below:

expecting perfection

This distortion involves having unrealistic expectations of perfection in one's life.

Distortion: In the world of social media, it may look like everyone leads perfect lives. Every time you look at your Instagram feed, you put down your phone feeling a bit depressed as you look at how everyone is living these exciting, vibrant lives—while also looking beautiful.

Reality: Social media shows the highlight reel of everyone's lives. Individuals can spend hours creating the "perfect" photo at the right angles while using filters to boost images. The truth is that this simply isn't anyone's reality.

self-defeating comparisons

This distortion involves inaccurately comparing ourselves to those who appear better off than us and putting ourselves down in the process.

Distortion: You look at your friend Aisha, and she is popular, smart, and pretty and seems to manage being in sports while having a ton of friends. She seems like she has it all, especially with her posts of vacations in exotic island locations.

Reality: Aisha's life may not be as ideal as you are observing from social media. Her parents may be having marital or financial difficulties, or she may be getting bullied by someone at school.

labeling

This distortion involves putting yourself down instead of finding ways of improving behavior for better results in life.

Distortion: Your parents keep giving you a hard time about being on your phone, while your friends just removed you from a group chat. You think, *I must be a total loser* and start isolating yourself in your bedroom.

Reality: Managing parental expectations and staying on good terms with friends can be challenging. It is possible that all the time on your phone is not only keeping you distracted while with your family but also unavailable emotionally to friends in real life.

magnification/minimization

This distortion involves discounting the good and overemphasizing the bad.

Distortion: Your phone just did an automatic update that lost all your fitness data. You become angry and stressed out (magnification).

You just set a running record on your fitness app and downplay what an accomplishment this was (minimization).

Reality: Fitness is good for us regardless of what our data does or does not say. Sometimes our devices can actually make the things we enjoy, such as running, stressful because of technological errors.

directions

Now that you have learned many different forms of thought distortions, see if you can come up with one example for each type of distortion below, using examples from your own life:

Black-and-white thinking (all-or-nothing)

_____

_____

_____

Catastrophizing

_____

_____

_____

Fortune telling (mind reading or predicting the future)

_____

_____

_____

Expecting perfection

_____

_____

_____

Self-defeating comparisons

_____

_____

_____

Labeling

_____

_____

_____

Magnification/minimization

_____

_____

_____

more to do...

In the last activity, you practiced the skill of identifying thoughts and coming up with alternative explanations. On the next page, you can bring all this knowledge and practice together by using a thought log. A thought log is made up of these components: a stressful scenario, a place to list feelings and automatic thoughts (typically distorted thoughts), as well as an alternative thought.

You can use the log on the next page any time you experience a stressor related to social media, devices, or other anxieties and walk yourself through ways of coping and objectively assessing your thoughts. At http://www.newharbinger.com/41900, you can download additional copies.

Stressful scenario: _____

Feelings	Automatic thoughts	Cognitive thought distortion	Alternative thought

when cyberbullying strikes 13

for you to know

According to statistics, over half of all adolescents report to being cyberbullied at one point in time. Approximately 25 percent of teens are cyberbullied on an ongoing basis. Given the accessibility and, often, anonymity of technology, cyberbullying is far too common with harmful consequences.

It is very likely that either you or someone you know has been harmed by cyberbullying. In fact, it's even possible that you contributed to the bullying of someone else without intending to. Cyberbullying is typically defined as involving either *verbal* (making harassing or threatening comments) or *relational* (for example, spreading rumors about someone) aggression.

With the rise of secondary Instagram accounts (Sinstas) and Snapchat, where messages can immediately disappear, cyberbullying can run rampant. Teens can make deprecating comments about one another on secondary social media accounts without parents ever finding out, and worse, in Snapchat or stories, the evidence is lost. Furthermore, statistics show that only 20 percent of cyberbullying is ever reported to parents. Though teens may not always grasp the gravity of the situation, there have been enough instances of bullying leading to suicides and self-harm to cause alarm. Members of marginalized groups such as racial minorities and LGBTQ teens have been particularly vulnerable to these outcomes. Learning to deal with cyberbullies is important to not only protect yourself but also help friends in need.

directions

Below are some of the common problems many teens run into on social media that can lead to cyberbullying. It is important to remember that no one deserves to be bullied and that no course of action justifies such behavior.

Cyberbully-Proof Your Life!

Use this checklist to help protect you and friends from being victims of cyberbullying. Check the ones you already do, and place an X for the ones that you can start to do in the coming days.

_____ Make sure you know everyone who requests you on social media. Even though many teens aspire to getting thousands of followers, it is not worth risking your safety.

_____ If a cyberbully tries to contact you, block them on all social media.

_____ If you are included in a negative post, do *not* comment. You may want to fight back, but that is what cyberbullies are looking for. Do not engage them!

_____ If you are a victim of cyberbullying, keep the evidence through screenshots and don't be afraid to report it to parents and school authorities.

_____ Limit your active involvement in social media. Even innocuous posts from celebrity Instagrammers quickly go sour, and commenters start attacking one another. Make life simpler by avoiding any comments whatsoever beyond a "like" or "love."

_____ Listen to your gut! If something seems off on social media or you think a friend might be starting to cyberbully you or someone you know, speak up. Tell a parent or confront the friend directly (off social media) if you feel comfortable, but don't let yourself become a victim!

---

more to do...

A major concern regarding cyberbullying is that many teens do not recognize its subtle signs before it is too late. They are so accustomed to social "drama" that when behaviors move to a more aggressive form (overt or passive-aggressive) they come to see these behaviors as normal. Not only that, but they then start to mimic these very actions and become cyberbullies themselves. Use the chart below to keep you and friends from spreading these toxic behaviors.

Don't Become a Cyberbully (or Let a Friend Become One)!

Below are some of the most common tactics cyberbullies use, according to the governmental organization StopBullying. Be as honest as you can, and check any behaviors you may have participated in.

____ Posting a mean or hurtful photo or video of someone

____ Posting comments or spreading rumors about someone that are embarrassing, mean, or hurtful in any way

____ Threatening to hurt someone or telling them that they should kill themself

____ Pretending to be someone else online to post personal or false information about someone else

____ Creating a mean or hurtful web page about someone else

____ Posting mean or hateful comments about someone based on their race, religion, ethnicity, or sexual orientation

---

After completing the two charts, answer the following questions below:

Have you ever been the victim of cyberbullying? What happened? Did it stop?

_____

_____

_____

_____

_____

_____

Have you ever been a perpetrator of cyberbullying? How did it happen? Did you make amends or apologize for the behavior?

_____

_____

_____

_____

After completing these activities, how might you change your online behaviors to protect yourself from online bullying and keep from being a bully to others?

_____

_____

_____

_____

getting bored on purpose 14

for you to know

It has been said that if necessity is the mother of invention, then boredom is its father. Recent studies suggest that a lack of free, unstructured time is leading to a decrease in creativity in youth. When left free to daydream, imagine, and create, teens are not only more content but more creative as well.

In recent years, experts have expressed concern over the lack of free time and creative play in children and teens. Being scheduled from a young age in sports, camps, and other activities has led to excess pressure and stress. Even activities that are well intentioned, such as art classes, often require sitting still, following step-by-step instructions, and sticking to some level of structure. How do teens learn to be completely free and uninhibited?

Our constant state of connection to our devices disrupts this natural flow of creativity and wonderment about the world. As soon as we start to feel bored and disengaged, we may be quick to turn to our devices and screens as a babysitter of sorts that keeps us occupied and entertained. But what happens when you put the technology away and let your mind roam free? While initially it may be uncomfortable, inviting yourself to experience good old-fashioned boredom can be highly instructive.

directions

During a time when you might ordinarily be tempted to idly look at your phone, watch a show on a device, or text friends, see if you can stop yourself and simply do nothing. Observe the discomfort or sense of feeling antsy that comes up for you. Resist the urge to tune out or plug in to something. Think about what other type of activity calls to you at this moment that does not involve a screen.

Perhaps you'd like to take a relaxing bath. Maybe you'd like to draw, paint, or pick up your guitar. Instead of spending thirty minutes watching a show or engaging in a screen-related activity, dedicate that same block of time to a personal interest of yours that evokes a sense of calm—for example, knitting, playing the violin, or getting lost in a yoga practice.

Pick one activity and allow yourself to get fully immersed in what psychologist Dr. Mihaly Csikszentmihalyi calls *flow*. We often experience flow when we are "in the zone" or are so immersed by an activity that we lose all track of time. Allow yourself to be thoroughly absorbed in the activity without the distraction of technology or disturbing alerts from your devices. You might even close your eyes and take a few deep breaths before allowing yourself to be fully absorbed in this meaningful activity.

As you engage in your activity, breathe in the feeling of joy and lightness you experience. You could even allow yourself to repeat this famous quote by the ancient poet Rumi as your own personal mantra: "Let yourself be silently drawn by the strange pull of what you really love." When the time comes to move on to another activity, be gentle, mindful, and intentional about the transition. Avoid abruptly jumping up, picking up your device, or quickly changing activities. Allow a few moments to gently breathe again, maybe close your eyes, and slowly make your way back to your reality.

Write down the activity you completed and add a few sentences on how you felt afterward. Note also any changes in mood before and after completing the activity.

_____

_____

_____

_____

_____

_____

more to do...

Learning to move off our devices takes time and observation. Perhaps you get bored during a TV show or waiting at the doctor's office. You will start to notice patterns in when you have idle time or become disengaged. Using the chart below, list the times of day and scenarios when you are likely to have idle time and how you typically spend the time. Then, come up with a new replacement activity in lieu of your old behaviors. Some examples are provided below.

Time of day	Old activity	New activity
First thing in the morning, while still in bed	Checking my social media feed	Taking a few slow, deep breaths and setting an intention for the day
During lunch at school	Playing games on my phone	Talking to friends or getting a head start on my homework
After school	Binge-watching a favorite television show	Working on my knitting skills while listening to music, or talking to my mom

Now, come up with examples from your own life:

Time of day	Old activity	New activity

distracting yourself...without devices 15

for you to know

Sometimes the best way to jump-start new behaviors or work on fresh goals is through finding new activities. Many times we can get into a rut, doing the same hobbies we used to enjoy but no longer deriving any pleasure from them. Branching out and trying new things can be an integral part of creating lasting change.

Most teens these days say they are too busy for hobbies. Between the many demands of school, friends, and other activities, they have very little time to themselves. What precious time they have left over often ends up being spent in sleep or doing an extra-credit assignment, or maybe a movie with friends if they're lucky. When they do end up with idle time, they almost instinctively go to their devices for entertainment. Phones and apps can be the ultimate escape for teens and are attractive as a result.

Distraction is a therapeutic technique that refers to replacing anxious thoughts with activities that will get our minds off the distressing scenario. Most teens are well acquainted with this technique, which they often know as "binge-watching Netflix." Although getting lost in a television show is certainly a way of unwinding, it is not the best way of unplugging and tapping into more active ways of coping.

On the pages that follow, you will find a list adapted from *The Dialectical Behavior Therapy Skills Workbook*. It includes over seventy different coping tools you can try when you need a break from social media and your devices. These tools can help you unplug, unwind, and reenergize, while introducing you to hobbies you may have forgotten all about. Although you might be tempted to do some of the hobbies using a device (for example, finding exercise videos on YouTube), challenge yourself to change up your surroundings—find an actual class at a gym!

directions

Below is a list of activities and potential ideas teens can turn to for coping. Place a check next to activities you already participate in and an X next to the ones you are willing to try, then add any other activities you can think of. For easy access, you can download this list at http://www.newharbinger.com/41900.

_____ Journal.

_____ Write a gratitude list.

_____ Go to a yoga studio and try out a new class.

_____ Create a sacred space and meditate.

_____ Go to a place of worship and pray.

_____ Visit a Buddhist center or other spiritual place.

_____ Go to a gym to exercise.

_____ Lift weights.

_____ Go swimming.

_____ Take a Pilates or spinning class.

_____ Ride your bike.

_____ Go for a hike or plan a hike.

_____ Go camping or plan a camping trip.

_____ Go skiing or snowboarding, or plan a trip to a local mountain.

_____ Dance in your room or take a class.

_____ Rebound/jump on a trampoline.

_____ Go for a run or jog outside.

_____ Take a slow, meditative walk outside in nature.

_____ Take a class in tai chi or qigong.

_____ Take your dog for a walk, or borrow a friend's dog and take it for a walk.

_____ Go outside for fresh air, even if you just sit on the front porch.

_____ Go outside and watch the birds, animals, and nature.

_____ Join a game being played at your local playground, or simply watch the game.

_____ Play a musical instrument or learn how to play one.

_____ Sing or learn how to sing.

_____ Write or compose a new song.

_____ Write a poem.

_____ Learn a new language.

_____ Listen to upbeat, happy music.

60

_____ Make a playlist of uplifting songs for when you might need it.

_____ Sing in a local choir.

_____ Participate in a local theater group.

_____ Go to the movies.

_____ Make a list of your top five funniest films to watch when feeling down.

_____ Join a club.

_____ Make a fresh cup of tea or coffee, or a smoothie, and drink it somewhere special.

_____ Go to a new coffee shop or a favorite one.

_____ Go to a bookstore or library.

_____ Go to the mall or other shopping center to window-shop.

_____ Visit an arts and crafts store for supplies to start a project.

_____ Knit or crochet, or learn how to.

_____ Make a scrapbook.

_____ Take photographs.

_____ Draw, color, or doodle in your sketchbook.

_____ Color a mandala or other meditative image.

_____ Visit an art museum.

_____ Create a new recipe and try it.

_____ Sign up for a cooking class.

_____ Go out for something to eat.

_____ Cook your favorite dish or meal.

_____ Bake cookies for a friend in need.

_____ Sign up to volunteer for a charitable organization.

_____ Plant a garden or visit one.

_____ Clean out your closet and donate clothes you no longer wear.

_____ Organize your bedroom.

_____ Light candles.

_____ Take a relaxing bath.

_____ Take a warm shower.

_____ Give yourself a facial.

_____ Polish your nails.

_____ Get or schedule a pedicure.

_____ Go to a sauna or steam room.

_____ Schedule a haircut or try a new hairstyle.

_____ Get a massage or rub your own feet.

_____ Do a puzzle with many pieces.

_____ Read a book.

_____ Reread your favorite book or series.

_____ Read a magazine.

_____ Sleep or take a nap.

_____ Eat dark chocolate. (It's good for you!)

_____ Make a list of ten things you appreciate about yourself or that you are good at (and look at this list when you feel blue).

_____ Write a loving letter to yourself when you are feeling good and read it to yourself when you're feeling upset.

_____ Make a vision board.

Other: _____

Other: _____

Other: _____

Other: _____

With this long list of ideas to try, it is likely you have some new ideas percolating about activities to try out. Pick two or three of these ideas, and try implementing them in the next week, then pick another two or three to try out the following week. List these activities below, and after doing each, rate your level of enjoyment on a scale of 1 to 10 by circling the corresponding number. Consider integrating the activities you enjoyed the most into your life on a regular basis.

Week 1:

Activities to try	Level of enjoyment									
1: _____	1	2	3	4	5	6	7	8	9	10
2: _____	1	2	3	4	5	6	7	8	9	10
3: _____	1	2	3	4	5	6	7	8	9	10

Week 2:

Activities to try	Level of enjoyment
1: _____	1 2 3 4 5 6 7 8 9 10
2: _____	1 2 3 4 5 6 7 8 9 10
3: _____	1 2 3 4 5 6 7 8 9 10

more to do...

When teens are bored or disengaged, they often avoid the situation through idle time on their phone. By creating a *coping kit*, you can have an easily accessible set of tools to use when you are feeling bored, anxious, or uneasy in any way. You can keep the items in a small backpack, purse, or even a ziplock plastic bag.

If any of the hobbies you marked were particularly inspiring and are portable (such as a sketchpad, journal, book, or puzzle), you might consider putting these items in your kit. You might also consider filling the bag with soothing things that bring you instant comfort; for example, a meditation coloring book with colored pencils, a book of inspiring quotes, a soothing stone to hold, relaxing teas, or a bottle of water.

When you're bored or antsy, you have the assurance of knowing you have a kit of tangible items to help you cope.

16 reading books, not screens

for you to know

Many teens report that during childhood they loved getting lost in books, but their interest waned in high school, when reading became mandatory and felt oppressive. Reading can be one of the best ways to distract yourself when stressed, or it can simply help you relax and give your mind a break.

Many teens report that most of their reading happens on screens. Additionally, some schools are now providing students with iPads and other devices with textbooks loaded onto them. Further, many parents are reading on Kindles, iPads, and other electronic screens. Although going paperless is certainly green and wonderful for the environment, there is also something engaging about flipping through actual pages, and being able to throw a novel into a beach tote, where the worst damage it could face is some crinkling due to water splashes. Many teens admit that they don't read for pleasure nearly as much as they'd like due to the demands of school. Or if they do read for fun, it's a quick BuzzFeed article or other short link they click on.

directions

Think back to the types of books or articles you used to love reading. Perhaps it was murder mysteries or a series of some type. Maybe you liked fantasy books about wizards and witches or those vampire teen dramas. Some teens like to reread entire series; others prefer to begin a fresh new adventure. Write down three different book titles or genres that you'd be interested in picking up in the next few weeks:

1. _____

2. _____

3. _____

Due to busy schedules, we may only be able to get to one or two novels in our spare time. But perhaps we can make time for magazines that we enjoy with more regularity. Maybe it's *National Geographic* or a celebrity gossip magazine that strikes your fancy. Food and home decorating magazines also count! Write down the names of three magazines that appeal to you. If you can't pick them up yourself, you could ask a parent to do it for you the next time they find themself at the grocery store or in a bookstore.

1. _____

2. _____

3. _____

Now pick one book and one magazine from your list, and over the next week, carve out some time to read this material. Perhaps you'll read a magazine over your cereal bowl in the morning and a few chapters of a suspense thriller before bed. You needn't worry about spending enormous amounts of time. Setting aside ten- to fifteen-minute blocks of reading time is a great way to start! After one week of reading, answer these questions:

What did it feel like to prioritize reading hard copies of books and magazines instead of reading for leisure on a screen or device?

_____

_____

_____

What were some advantages of reading printed material on pages instead of screens?

_____

_____

_____

Where were some disadvantages of hard-copy printed materials?

_____

_____

_____

Describe any differences you noticed in your emotions as a result of making time to read for pleasure. For example, did you feel less stressed, or more excited when getting lost in stories and articles?

_____

_____

_____

more to do...

Make it a priority to start integrating off-screen reading for leisure into your weekly routine. It can be a wonderful way to unwind and give your eyes a rest from being on a screen all day. You may even choose to integrate reading into your presleep routine (which will be discussed in Activity 17).

List three novels you'd be interested in reading for leisure in the coming weeks and even months:

_____

_____

_____

What changes might you consider making long term to integrate more time for pleasure reading?

_____

_____

What might be good days or times to prioritize reading for fun (for example, weekends, holidays, snow days)?

_____

_____

_____

How can friends and family help support you in reading more in print and off-screen?

_____

_____

17 sleep and blue lights

for you to know

Research indicates the blue light emitted from devices such as phones and computers can activate the brain, making it more challenging to fall asleep. Blue light–blocking technologies such as sunglasses and screen features help mitigate this effect. And beyond that, setting boundaries with phone usage at night can be an integral part of building good sleep habits.

Evening is one of the most challenging times to ask teens to give up their phones and other devices. That's the time when most teens text friends, have video calls, and browse their social media. Furthermore, research from the UCLA Sleep Center indicates that during puberty, teens experience "sleep phase delay," meaning that their bodies become sleepy approximately two hours later than before they entered puberty. So instead of becoming tired around eight or nine at night, they are still quite awake until ten or eleven. This change explains why so many teens report having difficulty sleeping any earlier than that time. With this new shift in a teen's sleep-wake cycle and the constant accessibility of phones, it is no wonder that bedtimes can creep later and later until well past midnight!

Research indicates that lights off at ten is ideal, given the important processes the body goes through in the earlier part of the night. These processes include melatonin production, stimulation of human growth hormone, and memory consolidation. Simply put, the quality of sleep in the earlier hours is more likely to impact how rested you are and ensure that the right hormones are helping repair your body and strengthen your immune functioning. The combination of lack of sleep, poor nutrition, insufficient exercise, and inadequate stress management can create an environment where the body is more vulnerable to contracting illnesses. This is why many teens are more susceptible to flu and cold viruses particularly after stressful events such as exams.

Unfortunately, screens that emit brain-stimulating blue light only further complicate matters. Most teens need computers to complete their homework and often stay up late writing papers and doing research. They are also endlessly available to friends, which means that when a text message comes in at two in the morning they wake up (if even asleep) and answer it. All these factors further harm a teen's ability to obtain solid sleep. Fortunately, learning to develop healthy "sleep hygiene" can help teens establish good sleep habits. Similar to good dental hygiene—which may include regular sequential steps such as brushing, flossing, and rinsing with mouthwash—sleep hygiene is also a step-by-step routine. The goal is to work backward from your typical sleep time to make sure all the steps can be completed in a timely sequence.

directions

Below are some of the components related to good sleep hygiene. Check the ones you already do, and put an X next to the ones you need to work on integrating. See if you can challenge yourself over the next week to maintain your healthy habits and add one or two new ideas each night.

_____ Avoid caffeinated foods and beverages (chocolate counts!) from four to six hours prior to sleep. If you are sensitive to excess sugar, also refrain from ingesting sugars several hours prior to sleep.

_____ Reserve your bed for sleep-related activities—no doing homework, checking email, or other such activities.

_____ If reading before bedtime is relaxing to you, consider doing this for ten or fifteen minutes. Choose material that will be calming and won't activate your mind. Read out of bed if possible; you do not want to spend too much time in bed doing nonsleep-related activities.

_____ Turn off all electronic devices or anything with a screen _two hours_ before bedtime.

_____ Activate any features your phone may have that keeps it from emitting blue light at night. On some phones this is called the "night shift" feature, and it allows you to set a time when the phone goes into this mode. This can also be a reminder of when you need to put away electronic devices.

_____ Find a comfortable temperature for sleep so that you are not too hot or cold to fall asleep. The ideal temperature for most people is between 65 and 72 degrees.

_____ Start preparing your body for sleep by slowly dimming the lights around you from one to two hours before sleep. This helps signal the body to start winding down for the evening.

_____ Take a warm bath or shower to relax your muscles one hour prior to sleep.

_____ Try a meditation, short prayer, or gentle stretches before bed. While ideally you won't sleep with a phone in your bedroom, there are some excellent apps that use yoga nidra (a type of sleep-related meditation), which can relax you prior to sleep onset.

_____ Do not go to bed hungry or overly full. Both scenarios can negatively impact sleep. There is some research that indicates the calcium and magnesium in dairy milk or yogurt can assist with sleep. However, if you abstain from dairy, consider a light snack if you're hungry and do not eat a large meal immediately before sleep.

_____ Try relaxing herbal teas prior to bed. Many stores sell chamomile or lavender teas that can help relax you. If you find a sleep-concoction tea, be sure to check with a doctor to make sure it is safe to ingest. Sometimes these blends include natural herbs that you may be allergic to.

_____ Avoid relying on over-the-counter medications or melatonin for sleep. The fact that you do not need a prescription for them does not make these sleep aids completely safe. Habits and addictions can form, so saving such medications for emergencies is a much safer bet.

_____ Try to have as much of a regular routine as possible so your body slowly becomes attuned to when it is time for sleep.

more to do...

Below is a sample plan for developing strong sleep hygiene.

4:00 p.m.	Get home from school, relax, and eat a snack.
5:00 p.m.	Start homework.
6:00 p.m.	Eat dinner with family.
7:00 p.m.	Finish last of homework.
8:00 p.m.	Take shower and start dimming lights.
9:00 p.m.	Read in bed or journal while drinking herbal tea.
10:00 p.m.	Lights out!

Use this blank chart to create your own custom routine. You can download additional copies at http://www.newharbinger.com/41900.

4:00 p.m.	
5:00 p.m.	
6:00 p.m.	
7:00 p.m.	
8:00 p.m.	
9:00 p.m.	
10:00 p.m.	

18 journaling instead of tweeting

for you to know

Research indicates the most commonly recommended intervention by therapists is journal writing. Taking time to write down our thoughts can be an extremely beneficial way of processing our concerns and realizing what truly worries us, and it can also be a way of finding answers and hope. Many teens find that a journal, whether they choose to write in it daily or not, can be a trusted companion they can turn to when feeling down or overwhelmed.

How many times have you been going about your day when suddenly an idea for a social media post popped up? Perhaps you took a funny picture or thought of a witty line. Or maybe you had a bad day and wanted to broadcast it to the Twitterverse in hopes of getting some positive feedback or comforting. It is natural when we spend so much of our time online to morph into thinking nearly nonstop in virtual terms. You go to a coffee shop and your latte art is so pretty you must snap a photo and share it with your friends. You are proud of yourself for making it to the gym, so you post a selfie standing next to the weights. It has become the common way of communicating with the world.

A decade ago teens would pick up the phone and run through everything they did that day with friends; today, they can show photos and update them every few minutes. It's like carrying your friends with you everywhere you go. Especially for teens who may not drive or have access to regular transportation, it can seem like a fantastic way of keeping up with friends and not falling behind on the latest news. However, one of the major downsides to this is that teens do not always learn to self-soothe.

Journaling is one of the most commonly recommended interventions because it not only helps promote self-soothing but also helps us process and discover new ways to view situations. Rather than reaching out to social media for support, being able to provide it for yourself is an invaluable skill. Selecting a special journal to record your thoughts can help facilitate this process. Perhaps a parent or friend gave you a journal as a gift one time, or maybe one caught your eye at a gift shop. Even though there are certainly online apps that serve as journals, most therapists recommend a paper journal, as the act of putting pen to paper has often been most reported by clients to be helpful. Also, because the goal is overall decreasing reliance on technology, a hard-copy journal is ideal.

directions

Experiment with keeping a journal, using this very workbook! If you need more space, feel free to use a special notebook you might already have. Reserve a few minutes (perhaps each night before going to bed) to jot down some reflections, fears, hopes, or dreams. Because journals may feel too open-ended for some teens, consider the following journaling ideas or prompts. Pick as many as feel right for you and commit to journaling daily for the next three or four days.

- Keep an art journal/sketchbook to draw your feelings, ideas, or thoughts.

- Keep a "gratitude journal," where you simply list three things you are grateful for each day.

- Use your journal as a space to write down every single worry and fear you possess, in the form of a brain dump.

- Make your journal a place to write down inspirational quotes you come across or positive affirmations about yourself. Each day, come up with a single quotation or affirmation.

- Write down a list of everything you did that day. It doesn't have to be long paragraphs, just a bulleted list of when you woke up, what you ate, what you did, whom you talked to, and so forth. You can choose a number from 1 to 10 to rate how you felt about the day (1 being terrible, 10 being excellent).

- Pick one of the goals you have been working toward in this workbook and write about how your progress is coming along. Tell how you might want to change things up to help you succeed.

- Write about your journey toward moving away from social media. Include any fears you may have or frustrations you may be feeling.

- If you are currently in therapy or meeting with a counselor, write down the things you might want to bring up at your next session. Doing that can help jog your memory regarding what you wanted to talk about.

_____

_____

_____

_____

_____

_____

_____

_____

_____

_____

_____

_____

_____

_____

more to do

At the end of your experiment with journaling, answer these questions:

Which prompts did you find yourself most drawn toward?

_____

_____

_____

_____

Write about any recurrent themes that came up in your journaling (for example, a troublesome issue in your life or anxious feelings).

_____

_____

_____

_____

Write about any positive impact the journaling process has had on your daily life.

_____

_____

_____

_____

_____

activity 18 ✳ journaling instead of tweeting

What commitment can you make to journaling on a regular basis? Would daily or even weekly journaling be feasible for you?

_____

_____

_____

Write down how often you would like to see yourself journaling and what type of journal you might keep (for example, sketchbook or gratitude journal). You might at this point even consider purchasing a special journal or notebook for regular use.

_____

_____

_____

_____

_____

_____

_____

exercising without earbuds 19

for you to know

Studies show that exercise can be just as effective in relieving the symptoms of depression as medication, and more effective over the long run. We all know exercise is good for us, but few realize how impactful it can be in improving our mental health. Learning to prioritize exercise is not only helpful for the physical body but also helps us sleep better and feel less affected by stressors.

You have probably already heard it many times before—in fact, more times than you'd like to count! "Exercise more!" "Just get outside and move; you'll feel better." "Go walk the dog; do *something*!" Many teens struggle with this basic building block of better self-care. Although at times you may feel like you lack the energy to devote to exercise, the reality is that integrating physical movement can significantly increase your energy. As an added benefit, exercise helps improve our sleep and manage our anxiety, because it is a wonderful break from the constant stimulation of everyday life. While gyms are often loud, pumping blaring music through loudspeakers, peaceful walks or jogs in nature can be highly restorative. On the other hand, if a loud music-driven Zumba class or a spin class is more up your alley, those are great too. Just make sure exercise is not used as a form of punishment, but rather a way to engage, detoxify, and de-stress.

The key to healthy, sustainable exercise patterns is to find the exercises that work best for you. For centuries, the Indian naturopathic healing practice known as Ayurveda has helped people find which form of exercise is right for their body type, and the practice has been picked up by modern-day experts. The idea behind this philosophy is that not every body type is optimally built to be a weight lifter, the same way not every body type is meant to be a ballerina. This is not to say people can't do an exercise not matched with their body type. Rather, these guidelines help shine a light on the variety of exercises that actually "count" as exercise.

directions

Below you will find three "clusters" of types of exercise based on the Ayurvedic principles of medicine. Adapted from the work of chiropractor and naturopathic medicine expert Dr. John Douillard, these clusters correspond to the three *doshas*, or body types. Using the chart that follows (or one downloaded from http://www .newharbinger.com/41900), circle all the activities that appeal to you. Notice whether the activities you enjoy or are drawn to conform more to one cluster than another.

Cluster 1	Cluster 2	Cluster 3
Activities that are slow and calming, and that help with rejuvenation (helpful for anxious types).	Activities geared toward those who are highly competitive and must exert stamina, speed, and strength.	Activities for those who are calm and do well under pressure. These require endurance and mind-body coordination.
Low-impact aerobics	Basketball (and other team sports)	Aerobics
Dance	Ice skating	Body-building
Bowling	Hockey	Soccer
Badminton	Kayaking	Gymnastics
Ballet	Skiing (downhill)	Shot put
Baseball	Surfing	Fencing
Swimming	Touch football	Javelin
Yoga	Windsurfing	Inline skating
Hiking	Waterskiing	Rowing
Golf	Mountain biking	Rock climbing
Doubles tennis	Diving	Tennis
Walking	Noncompetitive racquet sports	Volleyball
Horseback riding	Cross-country skiing (recreational)	Lacrosse
Martial arts	Golf	Handball
Weight training	Yoga	Cross-country running
Sailing		Stair-stepping
Ping-pong		Parkour

Next, list any types of exercise that you already participate in:

_____

_____

_____

_____

Over the next week, see if you can integrate one or more of these additional exercises into your regimen two or three times. Borrowing from the idea of SMART goals in Activity 6, list how many times a week you will engage in these activities, the duration, and any other pertinent details:

_____

_____

_____

_____

_____

more to do...

After a week of integrating these physical activities into your schedule, answer these questions:

How did engaging in exercise impact your overall mood?

_____

_____

_____

What type of moods did you experience as a result of exercise? Were they generally positive or negative?

_____

_____

_____

Which activities did you end up trying, and how many times were you able to exercise?

_____

_____

_____

How can you make more time for exercise in the future?

_____

_____

_____

Did you find yourself more interested in activities from one particular cluster? If so, which one, and why do you think those were of greater interest to you?

_____

_____

_____

In the context of decreasing your screen time, how can exercising more help you stay away from your devices?

_____

_____

_____

Many teens report that they wear earbuds for music while exercising or that they take their phone to the gym with them. How might you be able to stay away from your devices while exercising?

_____

_____

_____

20 tech time management

For many teens, their phones are their lifelines. Appointments, important phone numbers, and reminders help keep them on track and make sure they know where they are going and when they need to be there. Many therapy clients receive text message alerts of their appointments on a weekly basis, so naturally phones can be critical in keeping things straight. However, though phones can be helpful in this aspect, they can easily eat up our time as well. What was supposed to be a quick scroll down our Instagram feed quickly turns into hours. Between texting and chatting with friends virtually, pretty soon it's bedtime and no schoolwork of any kind has been completed. Where did the time go? Author and businessman Stephen Covey described a simple way of managing time, using what he calls a "time-management matrix." The matrix below shows four quadrants indicating the importance versus urgency of an item, along with corresponding examples.

	Urgent	Not urgent
Important	Math test tomorrow to study for	SAT exam in three months
Not important	Interruptions, emails, phone calls, some minor homework assignments	Watching television, browsing the internet

directions

Take some time to think about all the things on your to-do list. Consider using a paper planner rather than putting everything into your phone, and organize your week according to these principles. Maybe the SAT exam is months away, but you still need to get ready for it, while attending to more urgent tests and projects due much sooner. Fill out the quadrants below for a typical school day:

	Urgent	Not urgent
Important		
Not important		

Also, pay attention to how much time in a typical day gets wasted due to social media or phone time. Consider allocating a very short and discrete period of time (from thirty minutes to one hour) for these activities. An hour-by-hour planner or other form of day planner can help you organize your after-school time to make sure you are completing work, having time for play and adequate sleep, and then leaving time for all the distractions that social media may bring.

more to do...

Write down an action plan for the week using the matrix above; you can download additional copies at http://www.newharbinger.com/41900. Your plan may include a variety of tasks you'd like to complete for the week, ranging from doing laundry to studying for an important exam. Again, be sure to pay attention to how much time is sucked away by low-urgency and low-importance technology-related distractions that keep you away from the things that matter the most. In fact, your phone or other device's battery charge level might just be an indicator of how your priorities need to shift!

	High urgency and high importance	Low urgency and high importance	High urgency and low importance	Low urgency and low importance
Monday				
Tuesday				
Wednesday				
Thursday				
Friday				
Saturday				
Sunday				

After a week of using this matrix, write down your experience with this new time-management tool:

_____

_____

_____

_____

_____

self-care for social media overload 21

---

for you to know

Self-care is perhaps one of the most commonly used terms by psychotherapists, as it embodies one of the most important principles we can learn. Self-care involves being gentle with ourselves, nourishing our souls, and filling our gas tanks when they start heading toward empty. By learning to practice self-care, you can ensure that you have the energy and zest you need to live each day to the fullest.

For teens stressed out by the constant buzz of technology and social media, self-care can be a critical way of resetting and rejuvenating. One of the great beauties of self-care is that it can encompass different things for different people. Self-care can be writing in your journal while drinking tea and listening to soft music. Or self-care can be lighting candles and taking a bubble bath. There are no right or wrong ways to practice self-care, as long as they promote health, safety, and well-being. Think of self-care as those extra special touches or gestures you might typically reserve for a beloved pet or a little baby. Now imagine applying that same attention to yourself. This is the beginning of self-care.

Self-care author and expert Ashley Davis Bush categorizes self-care activities in several simple ways. She discusses the concept of *micro* self-care practices as the things we can do daily that can be highly effective in keeping us grounded and content. *Micro* self-care activities are divided into the following types: grounding, energizing, and relaxing.

grounding self-care practices

Grounding practices can be thought of as those that help us reconnect to our deepest selves. They can include the following:

- Drinking a cup of tea with warming spices (for example, ginger, cinnamon, turmeric)

- Connecting to nature by taking a walk in the park or simply going outside

- Tending to a garden or even an indoor plant

- Eastern practices such as tai chi, qigong, and yoga

- Gentle stretches that can be done at home on a mat or in your bed

- Using your five senses to connect to the present moment

energizing self-care practices

Energizing practices are those that help uplift us when we have been feeling overburdened by the demands of the world. These practices can energize but also soothe. Examples include:

- Active forms of yoga such as vinyasa or hatha

- A brisk walk in crisp air in the park, or taking a hike by a river or meadow

- Self-massage techniques that involve gentle tapping

- Singing

- Dancing

- Cleaning and decluttering a space

- Laughter! Keep a collection of stories, memes, or jokes for when stressed.

relaxing self-care practices

Relaxing self-care practices may be the ones we are most familiar with in our culture. You've probably seen images of a stressed-out individual soaking in a bath or at a spa. While these images may be readily available in your mind, the realm of self-care practices that are relaxing extend beyond those.

- Sleeping, resting, or taking a nap, even if only for ten to fifteen minutes

- Meditating, doing deep breathing, or sitting in silence

- Using water to unwind (for example, by taking a bath, lying by a pool, or trying out a float tank)

- Using a mandala coloring book designed for teens or adults

- Giving yourself a spa treatment

directions

Fill out this chart to come up with your own personalized plan of *micro* self-care strategies.

Micro Self-Care

In an effort to prioritize myself daily, I will commit to the following activities each week:

Grounding	Energizing	Relaxing

In an effort to set better boundaries so that I can practice self-care, I will also prioritize saying *no* when appropriate (for example, to excessive social engagements that zap my energy instead of lifting my spirits, or to volunteering for more extracurricular activities when my schedule is already full).

Areas where I will set limits:

_____

_____

Because self-care also involves taking care of myself through nourishing foods, exercise, and sleep, I will also focus on the following goals:

Nutrition: _____

Exercise: _____

Sleep: _____

---

more to do...

In addition to describing daily *micro* self-care strategies, Bush also shares the importance of *macro* self-care. She describes *macro* self-care as the bigger things we might do to practice self-care. These might include taking a yearly trip to local beach or lake, getting a professional pedicure instead of a DIY one, or getting a haircut every few months. These are the things that can refresh and energize us but that we are not likely to do on a daily basis. Although you can do them at any point during the year, often holiday and school breaks are more accessible to teens, as they have more free time to focus on this type of self-care. Below, fill out a plan for *macro* self-care.

Macro Self-Care

In an effort to take better care of myself, I plan to do the following forms of self-care over the next year on a quarterly basis:

Fall (Thanksgiving holiday): _____

_____

Winter (winter holiday): _____

_____

Spring (spring break): _____

_____

Summer (summer vacation): _____

_____

---

22 nourishing your body

for you to know

We have all heard of the term "emotional eating." Our feelings and how we treat our body are inextricably intertwined. While some people overeat in response to stressors, others miss hunger cues entirely. Learning to tune into your body's needs is not only healthy for your physical body but can help soothe emotions as well.

Parents of teens regularly report that the car ride home from school or the immediate moments after a teen arrives home by bus or walking are not always pleasant. Tired, hungry, and overstimulated from the day, many teens just want to flop on the couch, eat junk food, and remain comatose for several hours. They also don't want anyone to talk to them (unless it is friends via technology). Their irritability frequently stems from their basic needs not being met. Often it is a combination of a lack of sleep and inadequate nutrition. Some teens come home with half their lunches uneaten because they felt too stressed to eat at school. Essentially, they are running on insufficient sleep and no fuel. It is a surprise that they don't have complete meltdowns upon arriving home!

Adequate nutrition is an important part of the equation for keeping any teen healthy and able to deal with stressors they may face at school and/or on social media. Although some teens can become overzealous in their approach and count calories using apps such as MyFitnessPal, some knowledge of balanced nutrition is key. Most high school health classes cover the importance of proteins, avoiding processed foods, and inclusion of a healthy dose of fruits and vegetables. The significance of these staples has been known for some time. Whether a teen is going paleo, vegan, or pescatarian, not depriving themself is extremely important, as is the inclusion of plenty of nutrient-rich foods.

Many teens will find that working with a nutritionist can be particularly helpful in coming up with a rough idea of meals, as well as what their caloric intake should look like given their activity level. Talking to a medical doctor or nurse can be a good way of also ensuring you are not making any drastic changes that will negatively impact your body. In these days of ample online resources, many teens learn recipes and tips from bloggers or YouTubers. The idea of "meal-prep" days is also gaining popularity in these busy times, with many social media posts made by bloggers touting its advantages. Even though this workbook has focused on decreasing device time, this is a scenario where the benefits of modest use can help you launch healthy new habits.

directions

Over the next week, take some time to notice what you are eating in a day. The goal is *not* to count calories! Instead, you are looking to make sure you are eating enough and that the quality of foods is high as well. If you are prone to mindless eating, paying attention to serving sizes will also be helpful. Be as honest as you can. While we may have the tendency to highlight the best in our eating, we have to be completely transparent to be able to improve or sustain healthy eating.

Use the chart on the next page for tracking; you can download additional copies at http://www.newharbinger.com/41900. The inclusion of snacks is not intended to suggest that you must have three snacks per day. They are just provided as reminders of times when you may choose to have a small bite to boost your energy reserves. Also, note that the percentage or grams of macronutrients can easily be found on the wrapper or packaging of most foods, or can be looked up online.

	Mon	Tues	Wed	Thurs	Fri	Sat	Sun
Breakfast							
Midmorning snack							
Lunch							
Afternoon snack							
Dinner							
Postdinner snack							
Number of carbohydrate servings							
Number of protein servings							
Number of fat servings							

You may choose to color-code this chart to help you keep track of macronutrients: carbohydrates, proteins, and fats. Although the suggested amounts of these may vary depending on the individual, you want to be mindful of including foods from each of these categories. Getting carbohydrates can often be the fastest and easiest source of calories, as most breads, pastries, and snacks fall into this category. Proteins such as peanut butter, healthy low-sodium deli meats, and cheeses may take a bit more thought and planning to obtain while also avoiding heavily chemical-laden protein powders. Further, fats can be your friend, especially with avocado toast and coconut oil-infused treats!

After tracking foods and nutrition over the last week, reflect on what stood out the most to you or surprised you about your eating:

_____

_____

_____

Did you find yourself not eating enough, or eating more junk food than you realized?

_____

_____

_____

Teens often list a host of goals for healthier eating, ranging from drinking water instead of soda to cutting out caffeine and taking more vitamins. What would you like to try changing about your diet over the next few weeks or months?

_____

_____

_____

more to do...

The acronym HALT has been used by therapists as a means of promoting more mindful eating, because for many, mindless eating can occur out of boredom, fatigue, or frustration. When considering your motivation for eating, try asking yourself these questions:

H: Am I hungry?

A: Am I angry?

L: Am I lonely?

T: Am I tired?

If you find yourself prone to mindless eating, what scenarios tend to be triggers for that?

_____

_____

_____

Which elements of the HALT acronym speak to your experience the most?

_____

_____

_____

How could using such an acronym help make you a more mindful eater?

_____

_____

_____

nourishing your soul

for you to know

Research indicates some of the happiest people attribute their disposition to a satisfying spiritual life. This does not necessarily mean that they attend a weekly worship service. Instead, they have a spiritual connection or sense of greater purpose and meaning in their lives through their own unique spiritual practice.

If you've ever sat outside and looked up at the clouds in wonder, closed your eyes and basked in the sun, or stood at the edge of an ocean and gazed at the horizon, you've likely had a spiritual experience. It is that sense we get when we feel that the world is so much bigger than our problems. We realize the importance of making the best of each day, rather than spending our time feeling anxious or upset.

We may experience these spiritual moments in any number of ways. Many times they occur in nature. Other times they happen in a place of worship. Sometimes it is a piece of music, a chant, or lighting a candle that moves us so. Some of us have private spiritual practices, while others diligently attend a weekly service. Whether we believe in a higher power, God, or simply nature, feeling a connectedness to a larger whole has the ability to uplift and support us. We realize that the weight of the world is not on our shoulders alone, and that we are all on this earth together, working side by side to make it a better place.

When we are busy losing ourselves in the virtual world, we lose touch with the present moment. We are thinking about the future or past, our minds weaving elaborate stories. This is where prayer or meditation can be powerful. The real things we fear are often the ones we really hold no control over. We may not be able to change a medical diagnosis or heal a parent's troubled marriage, but we can pray or send positive healing thoughts to our bodies or those in need. Running away from these things and burying ourselves in our devices only temporarily takes away discomfort or pain. Confronting them head-on with the knowledge that there is a higher source to help us can be deeply comforting and healing.

directions

Take some time and reflect on what a spiritual practice means to you:

_____

_____

_____

Describe whether you currently have, or have ever had, a spiritual practice. What does or has this consisted of?

_____

_____

_____

If not, how do you feel about the prospect of integrating a spiritual side into your life?

_____

_____

_____

Many people confuse religion with spirituality. Do you find them to be the same in your life, or do you see some differences?

_____

_____

_____

Now, in the space below, draw a map of your own personal spiritual journey from the time you were born to this day. Perhaps you were born into a practice where you were baptized or confirmed; or if you were not part of a formal religious group maybe you experienced profound moments of spiritual connection the first time you picked up a violin, went camping, or wrote a personal poem. Feel free to include highs and lows, times when you felt particularly connected and other times where you felt lost and without grounding. Be as creative and detailed as you can.

more to do...

In the next two weeks, come up with three ways that you'd like to try to reconnect with and infuse spirituality into your life. It may involve something like meditation, yoga, visiting a place of worship, or reading a book of prayers or meditations.

1. _____

2. _____

3. _____

Write down dates and times to participate in these activities in your planner, and try them out! Then, consider journaling about the experience using the journal discussed in Activity 18.

Section III

Going Tech-Free

24 virtual world to real world

for you to know

Making any type of big change can lead to anxiety and discomfort. Learning to rate our fears can help us monitor these feelings and actively work on decreasing negative consequences. Rating our fears also helps us have a better sense of when things improve because we can see our change numerically in a concrete way.

The virtual world can be very alluring, given its ability to transport us away from the here and now and into a life filled with friends, fun, and entertainment. Particularly when school can already be stressful, such an escape is natural, and many teens fall into this trap regularly. The virtual world can make us feel any number of ways, from more popular to glamorous or trendy. We can craft our virtual personas to show the very best sides of ourselves and our lives, even when in reality things may not always be so rosy.

Transitioning into living in the real world full time can be an adjustment. It is so easy to check a feed, send a text, and be occupied even when we are already engaged in an activity such as eating, shopping, or cleaning. One of the major challenges of real-world life can be that we fear missing out on what is happening with friends. We may feel awkward or uncomfortable just standing there without something in our hands to fiddle with. Learning to identify your discomfort can be the first step in making sure you are able to follow through with the goals you set for yourself while minimizing negative reactions.

directions

List your top three concerns about spending less time in the virtual world. Additionally, rank your anxiety on a scale from 1 to 10 by circling the number that corresponds to each concern:

Concern #1: _____

Level of Anxiety Related to This Concern

1	2	3	4	5	6	7	8	9	10

(little or no anxiety at all)   (highly anxious)

Concern #2: _____

Level of Anxiety Related to This Concern

1	2	3	4	5	6	7	8	9	10

(little or no anxiety at all)   (highly anxious)

Concern #3: _____

Level of Anxiety Related to This Concern

1	2	3	4	5	6	7	8	9	10

(little or no anxiety at all)   (highly anxious)

In previous activities, you have learned a number of coping mechanisms including managing thought distortions (Activities 11 and 12), finding new hobbies (Activity 15), and self-care (Activity 21). Consider actively using these techniques when anxiety strikes. Also, continuing to rate your anxiety as you make changes can be highly informative to you and your therapist, parents, or other trusted adults who may be guiding you through this book.

more to do...

Use the rating scales below to continue checking in on your anxiety in the coming weeks and as you continue working through this book. You can download the form at http://www.newharbinger.com/41900. It is at this point that you will be proceeding at full throttle, making major changes to your device usage and cutting back significantly on your screen time. Taking the time to monitor your anxiety during this important phase can help cue you in to when you might need to engage in additional coping strategies.

Mood Rating

1	2	3	4	5	6	7	8	9	10

(little or no anxiety at all)　　　　　　　　　　　　　　　　　　　　　　　(highly anxious)

Week 1: _____ (Date)										
Week 2: _____ (Date)										
Week 3: _____ (Date)										
Week 4: _____ (Date)										
Week 5: _____ (Date)										
Week 6: _____ (Date)										
Week 7: _____ (Date)										
Week 8: _____ (Date)										

making time for friends 25

for you to know

Research has shown that those with strong social connections do better in the face of adversity, are healthier, and live longer. With such busy lives, teens can sometimes neglect their friendships, as they find it difficult to make the time to nurture these important relationships. However, as teens reach out and spend more face-to-face time with friends, they often notice that their symptoms of anxiety decrease and that they feel happier overall.

When teens begin to seriously consider taking time away from their phones and social media, one of their biggest concerns often involves how they will stay connected. Because most teens are crunched for time, text messages and social media can provide a sense of connection that doesn't take away from their busy schedules. Between the difficulties of coordinating rides to visit friends, sports, and after-school activities, many teens can go weeks without face-to-face conversations with friends. As such, the concept of eliminating devices can seem counterproductive for maintaining such friendships. Many teens report texting and social media save them the time of commuting back and forth to connect in person; furthermore, it is immediate communication!

Indeed, it can take more work to nurture relationships without the instantaneous nature of social media. However, teens often find that when they interact one-on-one with friends, the quality of interaction far exceeds those that occur virtually. The world of personal interactions is so much richer with experience, and most teens know this intuitively. Because it is far simpler to do what everyone else does—communicate with their devices— it can take more work and planning to break this cycle.

When given the challenge of finding something to do with their friends (that does not involve their phones!), most teens are not at a loss. They list a whole host of fun activities, but the real challenge is coordinating schedules. It can be frustrating to look at calendars and have to schedule an activity more than a week out. However, once you are in the habit of prioritizing activities with friends, things can become much more automatic and habitual.

directions

Activities with friends can take shape in a variety of forms. Some activities involve more planning, while others can be spontaneous and can occur after school on the bus back home. Thinking about activities in terms of level of time commitment (low, medium, high) can be an effective way of planning social activities with friends. In the chart that follows, list activities that involve low, medium, and high levels of time and planning. Then, integrate one from each category into your schedule over the next week. A few ideas from each category have already been provided to get you started!

Social Activities with Friends

Level of time commitment		
Low	Medium	High
Doing homework after school together	Organizing a sleepover party	Organizing and going on a road trip
Going to a coffee shop	Going to a movie	Going to a concert
Doing a puzzle	Shooting hoops	Planning a camping trip

After you have selected one activity from each section and integrated it into your schedule, answer these questions:

How did you distinguish between the types of activities you categorized as low, medium, or high?

_____

_____

_____

Looking back on the activities, how accurate was your judgment of how time-intensive each one would be? For example, did you find that an activity you thought was a lower time commitment ended up taking more time and planning than you expected?

_____

_____

_____

How would you describe your overall experience in trying out each of the three types of activities?

_____

_____

_____

_____

_____

more to do...

Think about what you can continue to do on a daily, weekly, or monthly basis to ensure that you continue connecting with friends. Using the chart on the next page, make a plan for the next month that includes ways you will prioritize face-to-face friend interaction time. You can download the blank chart at http://www.newharbinger.com/41900.

During especially busy times such as during final exams or midterms, how could you get creative about making time for friends?

_____

_____

_____

_____

_____

Month: _____

	Mon	Tues	Wed	Thurs	Fri	Sat	Sun
Week 1							
Week 2							
Week 3							
Week 4							

26 self-harm and social media

for you to know

Self-harm is more common among teens than many people realize. Although some teens who self-harm may feel suicidal, they often engage in these behaviors as a means of coping rather than an attempt to take their lives. Social media can serve as a trigger that worsens the urge to self-harm, and therefore examining the relationship between these two can be very important.

In stressful or difficult times, teens may engage in self-injurious behaviors, such as cutting, burning, or hitting themselves. Many teens describe the process of hurting themselves as something that is cathartic, as it takes away their emotional pain and allows them to "numb out." They often report engaging in self-harm when they feel they have no other options or ways to cope. In a very similar vein, when we mindlessly scroll through our social media feeds, we can also numb out. And many times, these two can go hand in hand.

Teens often report that they turn to their devices for support from friends and when they do not receive it, they may turn to self-harm. Or they may see something disturbing on social media, feel helpless, and then engage in hurting themselves. Learning to pay attention to how social media impacts your mood and propensity toward taking negative feelings out on your body is very important. Furthermore, some teens who have a history of self-harm report that they follow self-harm accounts on social media. These accounts may feature graphic images or encourage teens to continue this dangerous and unhealthy coping mechanism. As such, for teens who self-harm, it may be imperative that they stop following such accounts and start paying attention to situations that may trigger their urges. One helpful tool for decreasing urges to numb out by using devices or engaging in self-harm is mindfulness.

directions

One of the most commonly used acronyms for helping teens overcome the urge to self-harm or numb out involves the mindfulness principle of acceptance. The acronym ACCEPTS can help teens in times of distress become more grounded and mindful of the present moment instead of trying to escape it. Below, an example is provided for each letter of the acronym, along with a space for you to fill out an example from your own life:

A: Activities

Participating in hobbies, exercise, art, and music are all ways of distracting yourself from difficult emotions.

Write down an example of an activity you might engage in when tempted to numb out:

_____

_____

C: Contributions

Take your mind off your own worries and concerns by turning your focus and attention to ways you can help someone else or a cause; for example, volunteering for an organization or pet sitting for a neighbor.

Write down an example of a contribution you could make when feeling blue:

_____

_____

C: Comparisons

While social media encourages plenty of unhealthy comparisons, healthy comparison might help you see how others in similar situations may be coping in positive ways. Maybe you have a good friend or trusted older sibling or cousin who has experienced similar challenges as you. Comparing your situations and how you can integrate healthy coping tools can help you feel better.

Write down the name of a person or people in similar circumstances and what they are doing that is helping the situation. Then write down how this can help you work on healthier coping skills:

_____

_____

E: Emotions

Trying to evoke the opposite emotion of what we are currently feeling can sometimes help us snap out of a funk. Although you do not want to minimize true depressive or anxious feelings, sometimes you might just be feeling blue for no reason at all. Watch a quick, funny YouTube clip you love (being mindful of not numbing out on a screen for an extensive period of time), turn on upbeat music and dance, or do some cardio to get the endorphins pumping.

Write down what emotion you are trying to evoke and what you might do to accomplish this:

_____

_____

P: Pushing away

Mentally you might be able to push away the unwanted thoughts through a meditation practice where you focus on your breath, a mantra, or simply counting from one to ten over and over again. When you notice thoughts come up, you might imagine them floating up away in clouds across the sky or on leaves down a river.

Write down a type of imagery that can help you build a wall between you and the intrusive and difficult thoughts:

_____

_____

T: Thoughts

Distract your mind through activities that require you to think, whether it is reading, doing a puzzle, solving math problems, or memorizing lines for the school play.

Write down what type of thoughts might help you distract yourself from your challenging emotions:

_____

_____

S: Sensations

Tuning into your senses can help you if you are tempted to self-harm. Try holding ice in your hand, taking a warm bath, or smelling a pleasant lotion or essential oils.

Write down one way you can use your senses to help improve the moment:

_____

_____

more to do...

To continue practicing and integrating the principles of mindfulness into your daily life, you can further extend the ACCEPTS model by focusing in on the final step of the acronym. Many teens find that using their five senses further helps them as a grounding technique to use when they feel overwhelmed and tempted to self-harm or numb out. The examples that follow suggest how each of the five senses can promote a greater sense of mindfulness and calm. There is space for you to provide your own tools to use when needed.

Sight: One of the most common meditations that many people practice is a candle meditation. Focusing on the flame, they breathe deeply and calmly while mindfully observing the flickering movement. Other examples of using sight include taking a mindful walk and just noticing each tree and leaf, and even individual blades of grass.

Write down an example of how you might tune into your sense of sight to practice mindfulness:

_____

_____

_____

Smell: Perhaps the fastest sense to make an impact, our olfactory system is directly tied to our brains, making the memories of smell so powerful. Whether it is the smell of fresh cookies or newly cut grass, smell can be very instrumental in altering our mood.

Write down an olfactory memory and how you might be able to tune into your sense of smell to boost your mood:

_____

_____

_____

Sound: Whether it is the mesmerizing sound of a piano or listening to your favorite band, sound can immediately transport us, making us feel understood and supported. In contrast to sad music, which can intensify an unhappy mood, upbeat music can have us uncontrollably tapping our feet.

Write down how you might use your sense of sound to help you feel calmer and happier:

_____

_____

_____

Touch: Anyone who has stroked the soft fur of a beloved pet or other animal knows that feeling of warmth and the soft rise and fall of another living creature's breath. Touch can instantly make us feel connected to a larger whole.

Write down how you might use touch to feel grounded in the present moment:

_____

_____

_____

Taste: This sense has gotten many of us in trouble, as few things can be as comforting as a giant bowl of ice cream, chocolate, or freshly baked lemon bars. In moderation, taste can move us into a space of nourishing our bodies with healing foods.

Write down how you might use your sense of taste to help you feel more present:

_____

_____

_____

27 tech-free weekends

for you to know

Going tech-free is a movement that is becoming more common than you may realize. From famous celebrities to Instagram influencers, many people are speaking out publicly about putting their phones away to really start enjoying their weekends and free time.

Take a moment and think back to your childhood. Recall a memory from your youngest years when you were experiencing pure joy. In those early years of freedom, it was highly unlikely you had a phone. You met with friends on the block and spontaneously started a soccer game. Or you decided ahead of time that at noon you'd ride your bikes to the woods and go on an adventure. You weren't texting anyone to make this happen, nor were you hunched over your phone, typing away instead of being outside, experiencing life.

It is in this spirit that the tech-free weekend was born. Going tech-free is something we hear about more often, the more plugged into our devices we become. And now that you have been learning a host of valuable tools and skills for spending more and more time off your phone, it makes sense to take the final leap—a full weekend of no technology whatsoever! Although the idea may sound scary, stressful, or unreasonable, the rules for a tech-free weekend are simple. The time frame usually runs from Friday after school through Monday morning on a regular school week and can go much longer on a spring break or winter holiday. Anything other than items needing electricity (for example, your refrigerator) are off the entire period of time. This includes:

- turning off the television

- unplugging radios

- turning off cellular phones

- turning off computers

- unplugging iPads, iPods, MP3 players, and other such devices

Exercise trackers are also turned off!

How can you possibly make a tech-free weekend happen? Perhaps you've gone camping or on a day trip somewhere. Or if you were really fortunate, maybe you took an international trip on an airplane. You may have had no wireless reception for hours on end—and somehow you survived! You also managed to pass the time. On the car ride, you may have read an informational brochure or an old-fashioned paper map. On the airplane, you may have caught up on some sleep and kept yourself occupied reading a paperback novel. Referring back to the numerous coping tools and hobbies you've already developed through this workbook can also help.

directions

Talk to the people in your immediate family about how to facilitate a tech-free weekend. They might even be planning to talk you into such a weekend! Either way, having a plan is integral. Will you stay at home or go out of town? What are the rules and how are you all going to hold each other accountable? Remember, at the end of the day we are talking about a minimum of forty-eight hours. Perhaps you will finally find time to pick up that sketchbook or guitar again. It will be challenging at first, but as you get the hang of it, it won't be quite so difficult. You might even be able to implement a tech-free weekend once a month.

Use this form to write down your plan and intention for your tech-free weekend.

Date of planned tech-free weekend:

I will go tech-free for _____ hours.

Location of weekend (for example, at home, on a vacation): _____

_____

I plan to turn off the following devices: _____

_____

If I get the urge to use technology, I will engage in the following coping strategies:

_____

_____

During this period, I will focus my time and energy on pursuing the following plans, activities, or goals:

_____

_____

more to do...

During your tech-free weekend, consider using your journal from Activity 18 to record your thoughts and observations of how the weekend is going. Feel free to list any challenges, distress, and concerns you may be having. Also, if you are finding it to be liberating (which many teens won't admit to parents, but do report to therapists), write that down too! Then during times when you are heavily using your devices, you'll have a reminder of how freeing it was to be tech-free for a while. You may also consider rating any anxiety you may be experiencing, using the mood tracker from Activity 24.

After completing your technology-free weekend, use the space below to share some of your observations. What was most difficult? What went well? What, if anything, would you have done differently?

_____

_____

_____

_____

_____

Share your thoughts on doing another tech-free weekend in the future. When might you plan another one? (You can download a blank tech-free planner at http://www.newharbinger .com/41900.)

_____

_____

_____

Write down any new commitments or changes you are willing to make on a more permanent basis to further the momentum created by going tech-free for a weekend:

_____

_____

_____

28 "smart" vs. "dumb" phones

for you to know

Behavioral psychology treatments often focus on how behaviors can be changed through reinforcement or punishment, depending upon the circumstance. Most contemporary therapies don't rely on harsh punishments, so there is a common understanding that the best way to change habits is by removing temptations or altering the environment altogether.

Depending on how old you are or how long you've had a cell phone, you may have a hard time recalling life before one. Maybe you were nine when your parents gave you your very own phone, or perhaps you had to wait until middle or high school for such privileges. Some teens are given smartphones as holiday gifts or graduate to them after having had more basic phones. Either way, once you have had a smartphone, it can be difficult to imagine ever going back. When you can call, text, shop, check emails, take photos, check weather, order food, and find cheap gas all using your phone, why *would* you ever go back? However, when we become so dependent on one device to do everything for us, we can also feel hopelessly lost, anxious, and panicked without it.

In the previous activity, by going tech-free you were hopefully able to see what life is like without the constant buzzing and pinging of your devices demanding your constant attention. Perhaps life became somewhat less complicated and calmer. As an extension of that experiment, it can help to move down to a "dumb" phone for a few weeks. There are many ways you can move to a "dumb" phone. Here are some ideas to get you started:

- Use your existing phone, but have your parents turn off your data during designated periods of time. This way you can't access the internet or any apps.

- Ask a parent if you can use an old phone they once used. Unless they are exceptionally good at recycling, they may have an old flip phone lying around.

- Consider using a phone with only a keyboard for texting and no actual apps or internet accessibility; these phones look most like the old BlackBerry types of phones that are still sold at many phone retailers.

- Go to your local big box store (for example, Target or Walmart) and buy a prepaid phone to use for a week. These are typically less than twenty dollars, with no contract needed.

While many of the above ideas may sound involved, as you may have to visit a brick-and-mortar store, it can be well worth the inconvenience. For teens whose reliance on their devices borders on addictive, making a significant change like this can be the most effective treatment of all.

directions

Set up a time when your parent(s) are available to talk about making a change to your phone situation. Discuss what would make the most sense for you with respect to moving down to a "dumb" phone for a while. As you did when setting goals in Activity 6, be as specific as you can and have a timeline for how long this experiment will last. Fill out the box on the next page to help you make a plan to move to a "dumb" phone.

"Dumb" Phone Transition Plan

Goal: _____

Date I plan to move to a "dumb" phone: _____

Date I plan to visit a store to help with the transition (if applicable): _____

Phone features I plan to *use* during the transition:

☐ Making phone calls　　☐ Text messaging　　☐ Video calls/FaceTime

☐ Weather app　　　　　☐ Alarm app　　　　☐ Fitness apps

☐ Camera　　　　　　　☐ Social apps (for example, Instagram, Snapchat)

☐ School-related apps

Phone features I plan to *avoid* during the transition:

☐ Making phone calls　　☐ Text messaging　　☐ Video calls/FaceTime

☐ Weather app　　　　　☐ Alarm app　　　　☐ Fitness apps

☐ Camera　　　　　　　☐ Social apps (for example, Instagram, Snapchat)

☐ School-related apps

How long I will use the "dumb" phone for: _____

Coping tools I will use when feeling stressed by the transition: _____

_____

Tech-free tribe I can tap for social support during this time: _____

_____

more to do...

During your experiment with the "dumb" phone, write about the experience in the journal used in Activity 18, or record your observations below.

What did you find to be most challenging about the experiment?

_____

_____

_____

What was most liberating about it?

_____

_____

_____

Would you ever consider permanently using a "dumb" phone or making other permanent changes to your phone usage as a result of this experiment? Elaborate here:

_____

_____

_____

Following this experiment, what is one major takeaway that you can continue to apply to your daily life?

_____

_____

_____

29 developing self-compassion

for you to know

Setbacks are all too common when trying to reach new goals. Sometimes a major life event happens that we don't anticipate, or something smaller such as a brief illness gets us out of our healthy habits. We can become frustrated with ourselves for getting off track, but practicing self-compassion can help us get back there.

Many teens approach goals and new activities with zest and excitement. Given that the teenage years are all about trying new activities and finding your identity, it is easy to get frustrated when things don't work out as you anticipate. How many times has someone set a goal of eating healthier and succeeded until Thanksgiving and the holidays rolled around? Maybe you did really well putting your phone away, but then got a new job that required you to be on call. Or a teacher has you use an app for class, which brings back the temptations of getting on your device to use other apps. Setbacks happen to us all. What is most important is not beating ourselves up or losing hope. Practicing self-compassion can be an effective way of overcoming setbacks.

Self-compassion researcher Dr. Kristin Neff defines self-compassion as having three components:

- *self-kindness*, or avoiding harshly criticizing yourself;

- *recognizing your own humanity*, or realizing that all individuals have flaws, experience pain, and possess imperfections, as this is what makes us human;

- *mindfulness*, or possessing a nonjudgmental moment-to-moment awareness. When practicing mindfulness, we have a nonbiased experience of things whether they are painful or favorable, and we do not exaggerate or ignore them.

Self-compassion is not to be confused with self-esteem; the latter involves favorable self-evaluation whereas self-compassion is about self-acceptance regardless of consequences. Self-esteem may be built upon achievements and accomplishments, but self-compassion is accepting of failures and successes. According to Dr. Neff's research, two ways that you can actively practice self-compassion include journaling (Activity 18) and self-care (Activity 21).

directions

Spend a few minutes in meditation or prayer with a piece of paper and writing instrument next to you. Take some deep breaths, and spend some time tuning into your body and letting go of thoughts that come up. With each exhale, let go a little more and just breathe. Take ten slow inhales and exhales. Then imagine what it might look like for you to show yourself a greater sense of compassion. Envision yourself accepting yourself nonjudgmentally with all your flaws and weaknesses. Imagine a bright orb of glowing light surrounding you in unconditional love and acceptance. Breathe into this feeling. Take ten more slow, deep breaths. Then, gently open your eyes and write down what you saw and how you would define self-compassion for yourself:

_____

_____

_____

_____

_____

_____

_____

more to do...

To continue building resiliency against setbacks, consider the use of self-affirmations. Self-affirmations are brief quotes or words of inspiration to help lift you up in difficult times. You can find inspiration from favorite books or poems, or even just state something nice about yourself that you often forget. Find a sticky pad of notes, write an affirmation for each day, and place it on your bathroom mirror. Do this for a week, and journal about the experience in the notebook you used for Activity 18.

for you to know

Although it is common to get swept up in the stress of daily life, many teens find that when they take a step back to focus on their larger goals, they have a greater sense of purpose and meaning in their lives. However, regular demands on time can make it difficult to take small steps toward larger life goals. Redirecting time from social media and other devices and into goals can provide much satisfaction and hope.

First off, if you have worked your way sequentially through all the activities in this book, a joyous congratulations for making it this far! It is quite an undertaking indeed. It is also very likely that the same tenacity you applied to setting goals and making major changes carries over into other areas of your life. You may work hard at school, sports, music, art, social service, or any other number of areas. As such, you may have big hopes and dreams for how you want your life to turn out. One of the amazing things about the teenage years is that they are the dress rehearsal for adulthood. Teens can try on various costumes and roles until they find the one that fits perfectly (and even then, ideally they will continue to evolve and grow).

Perhaps through spending time engaging in self-care, hobbies, sleeping, and eating well, you have been able to develop greater clarity of mind. Or perhaps you have reacquainted yourself with past passions you gave up long ago. Wherever your journey has taken you, hopefully you have also come closer to understanding your visions and goals for your life overall. Anytime we take a break from social media and our devices, we find ourselves feeling lighter, less burdened, and happier. We start to see the connection between always being on and available on our devices and our increasing anxiety. We also start to notice how quickly we lose track of time when we are glued to our screens. Many teens report putting their phone down after twenty minutes of mindless scrolling and then wishing they'd spent their time better—doing yoga or reading a good book. It is a hard habit for us all to break.

Focusing on our wider goals can be an incredible way of reminding ourselves of what really matters in life. Our goals can be related to our careers or simply our vision of who we want to be one day. Whatever these goals may entail, chances are pretty good that we don't envision a lifetime of being a slave to our phones or computers. Moreover, our goals are about what we want, not what would make for a glamorous Instagram post.

directions

Make a vision board that illustrates your hopes and dreams for the future. Vision boards can be as elaborate or as simple as you'd like. Typically, you can use any type of posterboard or cardboard; then clip photos from magazines, quotes, or other items that inspire you, and paste them onto the board—basically like a Pinterest board, but in real life!

You can have photos of sports, a car you'd like to own, a college you'd like to attend, or an area where you'd like to vacation. Your vision board can be as detailed as you'd like it to be. Depending on how private it is, you might put it up in your room, or place it somewhere only you can see it.

If you feel stuck, you might just start by flipping through images in a magazine and see what calls to you. Maybe a photo of the ocean attracts your attention, jogging a memory of how much you enjoyed beach trips with friends. Or you see a photo of someone looking peaceful in meditation and you want more calmness in your life. It's even okay if your vision board includes something material you'd like to purchase one day, such as a pair of headphones.

The idea behind a vision board is that when we set an intention, it can become reality over time. Those who have created vision boards often report that the images they posted on their boards slowly have become reality. For example, they might post a photo of a meditating person to symbolize peace, only to find themself a regular student at a yoga studio months later. Or they might post a photo of a new car and get a pay raise that is a step in the direction of their dreams. To get you started, use the blank page that follows to cut and paste images, words, or any other inspiration that calls to you.

more to do...

Even though some of our greatest goals can take years to accomplish, there are often small steps that can help make them a reality. A student who is interested in a dream college might start going on campus tours, looking for high school internships held at that college, or learning about early admissions processes that can give them an advantage. If making varsity is a goal, then perhaps extra practices or at-home exercises might make a big impact. Remember, at the heart of this activity and those throughout this workbook is living your fullest life off the screen. So dream big! Don't focus on being the next Instagram star, but the star of your own life. Toward those goals, complete the following section:

Vision board goal #1: _____

(Write down one goal based on an image you chose.)

Steps I can take today toward that goal:

1. _____

2. _____

3. _____

Vision board goal #2: _____

(Write down one goal based on an image you chose.)

Steps I can take today toward that goal:

1. _____

2. _____

3. _____

making a pledge 31

for you to know

Putting pen to paper and signing our name under an oath can be a powerful statement. When our name is inscribed beneath such intentions, the commitment to change becomes much more personal. Many use a pledge as a way of declaring serious intention to change.

Perhaps at some point in your life you were asked to sign an oath or a pledge. It can be common in many high schools, for example, to ask students to sign a pledge promising they will never drink and get behind the wheel of a car. This request often follows a highly impactful presentation or testimony by a survivor of drunk driving. The beauty in this practice is that it signifies a desire from within to take a stance or make a change. It is not something to be forced upon anyone, and it allows teens to be truly authentic in their intentions.

Thus far, you have been provided a number of activities aimed at clarifying goals, obtaining support, identifying triggers, and managing anxiety. The final step to committing to change, whether you are doing this as a part of therapy or working through this book with a parent or counselor, is to write down your personal pledge and sign your name to it. Given that this workbook has primarily focused on decreasing social media and device usage while providing stress-reduction tools, it might help to include these in your pledge. Perhaps you'll include an intention for integrating more hobbies (Activity 15), exercise (Activity 19), or spiritual goals (Activity 23) into your life. Perhaps you will plan more tech-free weekends (Activity 27). At the end of the day, you want your pledge to speak to the multitudinous ways you intend to grow and thrive!

directions

Write your personal pledge below and consider having a trusted adult, such as a parent or therapist, cosign the pledge with you:

I _____ vow to:
                                    (name)

_____

_____

_____

_____

_____

_____

_____

_____   _____
            Your Signature   Date

_____   _____
              Cosigner   Date

more to do...

Celebrate! It is a huge accomplishment to have come this far and dedicated so much time to making big changes in your social media use. Making a pledge can be the final step in sealing these amazing intentions. As such, it can be important to celebrate this milestone in a way that is meaningful to you. Whatever you choose, finding a way to mark this special journey is an important step in reiterating the significance of the changes you have made and the amazing goals ahead.

Hopefully this workbook has helped you make some big changes in getting back more of your time and living a richer life. For so many teens, it is easy to get lost in the alluring world of screens. Any time we experience a negative emotion or concern, we can bypass the pain and go straight to enjoyment with the scroll of our thumbs. In many ways, our social media is the newest drug, and our excessive time spent on it can easily mimic an addiction. However, taking steps to evaluate your time and goals is critical in regaining the zest of your teenage years.

Throughout this workbook you have learned to manage your anxiety (Activities 11 and 12) and develop new hobbies beyond your screen (Activity 15), while focusing on improving your sleep (Activity 17), exercise (Activity 19), and nutrition (Activity 22).

Although it may be tempting to find yourself in idle moments going back to your devices, remember the mindfulness skills you have learned to deal with these times (Activities 14 and 26). Also, you may find some solace in knowing that you can reach out to family (Activity 7) and friends (Activity 8) to help support you, ideally in face-to-face interactions, whenever life becomes challenging.

Although you may find periods of time when you are doing exceptionally well at putting away your devices, it is easy to be swept back up into old habits. At those times, don't be shy about reassessing your time spent on devices (Activities 1 and 3). Apps that track time can help keep you accountable for how much time you are spending on your screens.

Although the advantages of technology certainly cannot be denied, the reality is that it is about finding a healthy state of balance. Technology can be wonderful when we can instantly see how many miles we jogged or log in to check our grades or assignments we need to complete. Certainly many areas of life have become easier because of technology: how convenient that we can book appointments for a haircut, deposit a check, or even consult with a doctor on our phones. But learning what to limit and when to limit your time is a skill you will continue to hone.

When you obtain your first job, you may need to be accessible by phone to your boss. When you go off to attend college, your parents may want to keep in touch through text. Although we cannot simply dump our phones, we can learn to allow them into our lives mindfully and intentionally. In special times, it can actually become more critical than ever to put these devices away. Although we may want to use the camera feature of our phones on graduation day, for example, we might also open ourselves up to getting unwanted messages. Many teens can relate to countless times when a single mean-spirited comment unexpectedly came through on a device and ruined an entire day that was meant to be incredibly special. So be vigilant to protect yourself and these moments.

Some simple food for thought—some indigenous groups have historically avoided being photographed in the belief that each photo steals away a part of one's soul. Meanwhile, statistics indicate nearly ninety-three million selfies taken globally daily, with one thousand selfies posted to Instagram every ten seconds. Although you don't have to strictly adhere to either mentality, you may consider putting the phone down and simply taking in more moments, capturing and savoring the images in your mind. Many times we are so caught up documenting that we stop fully living. So try your best to remember to simply be present and mindful, slide your ringer to off and your device to airplane mode, and get ready to soar!

references

Bush, A. D. 2015. *Simple Self-Care for Therapists: Restorative Practices to Weave Through Your Workday.* New York: W.W. Norton & Company.

Covey, S. R. 2004. *The 7 Habits of Highly Effective People.* New York: Free Press.

Csikszentmihalyi, M. 2008. *Flow: The Psychology of Optimal Experience.* New York: HarperCollins.

Douillard, J. 2018. The Best Workout for Your Body Type. John Douillard's LifeSpa. Retrieved April 7, 2018, from https://lifespa.com/ayurvedic-fitness-and-body-types

Lenhart, A., Pew Research Center. 2015. "Teens, Social Media and Technology Overview 2015." Retrieved April 7, 2018, from http://www.pewinternet.org/2015/04/09/teens-social-media-technology-2015

McKay, M., J. C. Wood, and J. Brantley. 2007. *The Dialectical Behavior Therapy Skills Workbook: Practical DBT Exercises for Learning Mindfulness, Interpersonal Effectiveness, Emotion Regulation & Distress Tolerance.* Oakland, CA: New Harbinger Publications.

Neff, K. D. 2003. "The Development and Validation of a Scale to Measure Self-Compassion." *Self and Identity* 2(3): 223–250. doi:10.1080/15298860309027.

Prevent Cyberbullying. Retrieved April 7, 2018, from https://www.stopbullying.gov/cyberbullying/prevention/index.html.

Prochaska, J. O., C. C. DiClemente, and J. C. Norcross. 1992. "In Search of How People Change: Applications to Addictive Behavior." *American Psychologist* 47: 1102–1114. doi:10.1037/0003–066X.47.9.1102.

Sleep and Teens. Retrieved April 7, 2018, from http://sleepcenter.ucla.edu/sleep-and-teens.

Goali Saedi Bocci, PhD, is a licensed clinical psychologist in private practice, published author, millennial expert, TEDx speaker, and media personality. She earned a PhD in clinical psychology from the University of Notre Dame; and completed her internship at the University of California, Berkeley; followed by a fellowship at Stanford University. Bocci has been a columnist for *Psychology Today*, writing the *Millennial Media* blog for nearly a decade, and garnering over two million hits worldwide. She is also a highly sought-after expert for top media outlets including *TIME*, *Newsweek*, ABCNews, *Chicago Tribune*, *Cosmopolitan*, *Refinery29*, *Elle*, and *Glamour*; and has served as a recurring guest on the morning television show *AM Northwest*.

You can find more information about her at http://www.drgoali.com.

Foreword writer **Gina M. Biegel, MA, LMFT**, is a psychotherapist, researcher, speaker, and author in the San Francisco Bay Area who specializes in mindfulness-based work with adolescents. An expert and pioneer in bringing mindfulness-based approaches to youth, she is author of *Be Mindful and Stress Less*, *The Stress Reduction Workbook for Teens*, and the *Be Mindful Card Deck for Teens*.

For more information, visit her website at http://www.stressedteens.com.

More ⏱ Instant Help Books for Teens

An Imprint of New Harbinger Publications

**THE PERFECTIONISM
WORKBOOK FOR TEENS**

Activities to Help You Reduce
Anxiety & Get Things Done

978-1626254541 / US $16.95

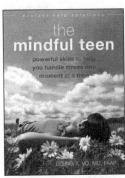

THE MINDFUL TEEN

Powerful Skills to Help You Handle
Stress One Moment at a Time

978-1626250802 / US $16.95

**THE TEEN GIRL'S
SURVIVAL GUIDE**

Ten Tips for Making Friends,
Avoiding Drama & Coping with
Social Stress

978-1626253063 / US $16.95

**THE ANXIETY WORKBOOK
FOR TEENS**

Activities to Help You Deal with
Anxiety & Worry

978-1572246034 / US $14.95

**A TEEN'S GUIDE TO GETTING
STUFF DONE**

Discover Your Procrastination Type,
Stop Putting Things Off & Reach
Your Goals

978-1626255876 / US $16.95

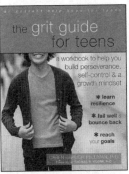

THE GRIT GUIDE FOR TEENS

A Workbook to Help You Build
Perseverance, Self-Control &
a Growth Mindset

978-1626258563 / US $16.95

newharbingerpublications
1-800-748-6273 / newharbinger.com

(VISA, MC, AMEX / prices subject to change without notice)

Follow Us 📘 🐦 📷 📌

Don't miss out on new books in the subjects that interest you.
Sign up for our **Book Alerts** at **newharbinger.com/bookalerts**

Register your **new harbinger** titles for additional benefits!

When you register your **new harbinger** title— purchased in any format, from any source—you get access to benefits like the following:

- Downloadable accessories like printable worksheets and extra content

- Instructional videos and audio files

- Information about updates, corrections, and new editions

Not every title has accessories, but we're adding new material all the time.

Access free accessories in 3 easy steps:

1. Sign in at NewHarbinger.com (or **register** to create an account).

2. Click on **register a book**. Search for your title and click the **register** button when it appears.

3. Click on the **book cover or title** to go to its details page. Click on **accessories** to view and access files.

That's all there is to it!

If you need help, visit:

NewHarbinger.com/accessories

new harbinger
CELEBRATING
40 YEARS